Falling Off the Roof of the World

The Autobiography of the Venerable Lama Dudjom Dorjee

Copyright © 2006 by Lama Dudjom Dorjee

ISBN 0-7414-3430-X

Published by:

INFIꙨITY
PUBLISHING.COM

1094 New DeHaven Street, Suite 100
West Conshohocken, PA 19428-2713
Info@buybooksontheweb.com
www.buybooksontheweb.com
Toll-free (877) BUY BOOK
Local Phone (610) 941-9999
Fax (610) 941-9959

Printed in the United States of America

Printed on Recycled Paper

Published September 2006

Acknowledgments

This book manifested first and foremost through the blessings of the three Jewels. Their presence in my life since the day of my birth has been a light, teacher, and guide in all my inner and outer journeys.

It is through their blessings that the right people appeared with the right skills to carry out the project. I would like to thank Ben Koch for his persistence, dedication, and wisdom throughout the many cycles of transcribing, composing, and editing the manuscript and for his managing of many details of the project; the Koch family for their patience and support through countless trips to "Lama-La's" house; Lori Benjamin-Rasor for her feedback and skillful editing of the manuscript; Kathryn Bodinson for transcription and editing of several sections; Larry Keenan for his editing and preparation of most of the photographs; Beth Keenan for her thorough research and design of the book itself; Julie Markle for her quick, fantastic work at indexing the book; Bruce Roe for additional editing; Susan Swaim for the design of the cover; and my wife, Tashi Chotso, and daughter, Tashi Dolkar, for their patience, support, and inspiration throughout the project.

~ Contents ~

Part 1: A Nomad Childhood

Born in the Shadow of Pa-ji-ri

According to my mother, when I took birth and entered this realm of being, it was early morning and the golden rays of the sun were just grazing the snowy tips of the mountain peaks behind us.

I arrived safely and soundly, but my mother often told me I cried quite a bit—more than my other siblings ever would. In Tibetan tradition there are many signs associated with one's birth that relate to its auspiciousness. For example, if someone is born at dawn it's more auspicious than being born at dusk, or even at night. And in general, being born in the daytime is better than being born at night. There is also the belief that certain days of the month are more auspicious than others, and so forth. These beliefs are steeped in the traditions passed down over centuries. Luckily, she also emphasized the fact that from the time I was born, no more children died in our family. My parents' first child didn't survive for some reason—he died when he was one or two years old. My father and mother were very sad about losing their first child, so they were a little extra worried about the second one—me. In the West today we might take for granted that most infants survive and become healthy children, but on the isolated plateau of Tibet, far from hospitals and delivery rooms bustling with doctors and nurses and machines, having most of your children survive is extremely fortunate. For my mother this simple fact was always a great blessing and she would tell me I was a "good boy." "No one died once you came."

In Tibetan culture they also believe that the environment in which you are born will influence, or reflect, your personality and the direction of your life—such as how powerful, gifted, or prosperous a person you will be, and so forth. A formidable mountain called Pa-ji-ri served as the environmental and spiritual guide in the background of my birth. My mother often told me I would be a strong and unique personality—a man who possessed the trait of self-reliance, of standing on my own two feet and thriving. Were her praises only the words of a doting mother, or did they reflect a more profound truth? I will let you decide, as you follow my life on this journey from the roof of the world across the great blue earth.

The Constant Melodies of Mantra

I was born in a Buddhist family. A spiritual mindset and outlook pervaded our lives, manifesting itself in the form of sweet melodies from the chanting and recitation of mantras. In Tibetan culture, even while one is doing something as mundane as milking a yak he or she will be reciting mantras. Men hauling yak dung and drying it for firewood recite mantras, and that tradition continues still today, even after the communists took over. You may have to recite more silently these days, but as long as you are reciting quietly, they won't know. You keep the practice more secret.

In the deepest part of my heart I remember my family nestled into our huge black yak-hair tent. Inside butter lamps flickered in each corner and a fire crackled in the center. The whole family would gather there to recite mantra and do puja (Buddhist prayers) in the morning and evening, but especially in the evening. There within the warmth and intimacy of the family tent, we would do special group practices together. Afterward, we'd tell stories and share our thoughts and dreams with each other. These evenings were very special.

A trusty yak, with a nomad family's yak-hair tent in the background

The Beauty of Our Yak-Hair Tent, Surrounded by Animals

Anywhere from two to five families traveled and lived side-by-side with us. You can imagine a small valley dotted with these 5 families, where we'd have our yak hair tents spread out. Let me tell you, yak hair is 10 times stronger than cotton or any other material, and if I remember correctly, a yak hair tent lasts from 5 to 10 years. It can handle rain and snow, but you do need to clear the heavy snow off the tent before it collapses.

My family's warmth extended beyond the inside of the tent. Outside, hundreds of yaks slept peacefully on one side of the tent. Their dark shaggy bodies covered the earth, and there the landscape seemed to be painted blacker than night itself. On the other side of the tent slept hundreds, or sometimes thousands, of sheep, their bright, white bodies dotting the earth like a gigantic mosaic. At night, in the glow of the crystal moon, a plush white rug seemed to spread for miles.

Our dogs kept an eye on everything. Every family had several dogs, who were depended on as unfailing guards and protectors. Some were completely fearless when it came to protecting their camp. They weren't bloodthirsty or anything, but they would jump at an unknown person approaching the camp even if he was holding a knife. Dogs were such beloved and valuable parts of the family that losing one was very difficult. I remember falling asleep to the patter of their paws and even to their barking and yelping as they patrolled our camp through the night.

Yaks loaded up and on the move. A family might need as many as 30 yaks to carry all of their belongings.

A Life of Constant Movement

As nomads, we were always moving. We moved from winter spots to summer spots, and sometimes we moved every other month in order to graze the animals. When we moved, we made large backpacks to load onto the backs of the male yaks. The average family needed 30 to 50 yaks to carry their entire load.

Some people would concentrate on herding the yaks during the move, some would herd the goats and the sheep, and some would ride the horses and keep an eye on everything. As for the dogs, they just followed along on their own. Because I was very small, I was strapped snugly to the back of a yak, or sometimes to the back of a horse, so I wouldn't fall off and get trampled. I have a clear memory of the view from the back of an animal carrying me: a sea of animals and people trailing along in groups behind me, all moving in the same direction.

When we reached our destination there was always a contest between families to see who could be the first to be all set up drinking tea. As soon as we got where we were going, the yaks had to be unloaded, the tents put up, and wood and dried yak dung gathered for a fire. Then, in order to win the contest, tea had to be prepared and served to the entire family. Everything was set up very quickly, before it could rain or get dark.

You might think that moving all the time would become tiresome, but as a child, I thought this type of life was very special. Looking back now, I see that the nomad form of transportation was very simple and peaceful, not to mention more natural and less harmful to the earth than modern transportation.

A typically beautiful—but powerful—river that nomads must cross without a bridge.

The 3 Ways to Cross a Raging River

Nomads in Tibet always have big rivers to cross; in the wide expanse of the Tibetan plateau, bridges were not a luxury we could rely upon. When we had to cross a deep river, I was always tied to one of the strongest, heftiest yaks and my legs would get soaked by the cold, rushing current as it crossed. I can still see the yak's back and those two horns poking up out of the water as we swam across. Each yak carried up to two hundred pounds, but that didn't keep them from swimming smoothly and almost effortlessly to the other side. These crossings were thrilling—and also terrifying!

Another way to cross big rivers without a bridge is by creating a device out of ropes and a large bucket. To make it you lay long, sturdy ropes from one side of the river to the other and attach a big bucket to them. One person gets into the bucket, and then you send the bucket to the other side, where somebody else is there to catch it and help the person out. Then you send the empty bucket back across and it is the next person's turn, and so on.

Another way we crossed rivers was by using a DRU-KO—a boat assembled by stretching dried yak skins across a wooden frame. This served as a small boat that could carry people or loads of things we wanted to keep dry. The raft moved downstream a bit as we crossed, but it did get us across safely.

But hanging onto a horse or a yak was by far the most exciting way to cross a river. The problem was that the river was usually so strong that the animal would be carried 100 or 200 feet downstream. Only the tip of its ears, and a little bit of its mouth, would be above water— the rest was underwater, so naturally you would be underwater too, holding on for your dear life. In those moments it was hard to tell if you were still on the animal or floating in the water, but you would hang on, and barely make it across to the other side. It was quite exhilarating. All your clothes would be soaked, but when you had made it across with your life, you didn't worry so much about your clothes!

No one said these Tibetan forms of transportation were easy, but when you wanted to cross a river, these were the things that were in store for you.

The Tibetan Family Unit

Looking back, I always rejoice that I had a family who, despite undergoing great trials and difficulties, always found strength to overcome the obstacles we faced in our daily lives and in the great struggles that would sweep across Tibet.

The importance of a strong, loving family is that it provides a stable structure upon which modern civilization can safely expand. If we can't even develop our own inherent qualities in order to bring our family into harmony and unity, how can we hope to govern cities and countries?

For this and other reasons I miss the Tibetan family unit I remember from my childhood. Very simply, we spent a lot of quality time together. There were really no arguments or fighting or major disagreements. Although we had limited resources, we also had limited desire for unnecessary luxuries. You could say we didn't have any desire for those things because we didn't know what we were supposed to be missing! But in the West today, we have so many new things flashing for our attention on a daily basis that our desire grows more and more, and that doesn't really help our situation at all. Actually, it creates more problems. Whether you agree with me or not, that's what I see, and that's what I feel when I look back and compare today with my childhood. I'm not saying it's good or bad, but that is how it happens—the more we have, the more we feel we need. The logical consequence is that we suffer more, because we always need more, and never find a state of contentment.

Anyway, when I look at mine and other Tibetan families, that strong family unit, a very important factor was that we didn't have TV or telephones, and in some ways that gave us more time for each other. But also, older siblings took responsibility for younger siblings. That helps a family tremendously. It seemed like the only thing mothers did on their own was give birth, and from that point on bringing up a child was a total team effort. My wife and I really missed that when we had a child in America. We didn't have that extended family support from a Grandpa and Grandma, from brothers and sisters, or anybody else. In Tibet you get so much help raising your child that you almost start to miss him! You almost have lay claim to him again and say at some point, "Give me my child back!" When kids grow up with that kind of love and care, they will bring that quality and that experience to their own kids and families.

I'm not saying Tibetans don't fight or anything, but I think there's a big difference between what you see now in the West and then. In those days of my childhood I don't remember much fighting. For example I just don't remember the idea of teenagers having problems with the family. I'm sure it existed at some level within Tibetan society, but very little. These days it is very different. If you take a look at young Tibetan teenagers born in India, Nepal, Canada, Japan, Switzerland, and America, I'm pretty sure they are learning modern ways real fast. They are getting blessings and transmissions from the country where they are being raised, so it's a little different now.

Surviving the Brutal Blizzards of Winter

Sometimes it snowed continuously for many weeks, with howling blizzard winds and avalanches dumping mounds of snow from different mountainsides. It made it impossible for the animals to go out, so we kept them all walled in, in a compound made of yak dung and rocks. This shelter shielded them from the cold and also protected them from wild animals. The horses and the baby animals were kept inside stables to protect them from the snow, and we always had hay and grain in storage to feed them. Before breakfast each morning, I would run out and check on all the animals, including the sheep, the yaks, and the horses, but especially the baby animals, who were my special playmates. I would even share my own food with them, which would get me in big trouble if my mother ever found me doing it!

These hardships of winter made it difficult to go far, which meant that it gave our family a chance to be together for extended periods of time. Without television, radio, movies or any other Western entertainment to occupy our time, we told stories, played games, built snow houses, went skating on the ice, and made designs in the snow.

Tibetan Social Security

My parents' attitude toward me and my siblings was always one of tenderness and devotion. In Tibetan culture the attitude towards our parents is based on a clear understanding of and appreciation for all the time and care they have devoted to our upbringing. As parents love and care for us when we are young and helpless, so it is unthinkable for us to send them to live elsewhere when they become old and helpless. We return the care we received with the same stable affection and loving kindness they gave us. You might call this the Tibetan social security system! Over the centuries it has been pretty effective and dependable.

My dear mother, Chodun Dorjee.
She did everything and anything to sustain us, even in the most difficult times.

My Mother: Heart-Light of Great Compassion

My mother's name was Chodun Dorjee. She gave our family support and structure within the home, managing the daily routine, as well as the cooking, cleaning, care of the yak and sheep, and the health and welfare of us all. Whenever there was a moment of poverty or difficulty, she gave everything and anything to sustain us. One brutal winter my brothers and I were suffering terribly from the cold. In Tibet, we wore long boots made from wool felt with a leather sole. Once these boots get wet, they freeze, and without some kind of insulation, we could end up with severe frostbite. Our mother had nothing but hay to stuff into our boots to insulate them. This kept us warm, but unfortunately the hay got wet and was never good for more than one day. To solve this problem, my mother would sleep with the wet hay close to her warm body each night. By morning she would have dry hay to put back into our boots. This kind of sacrifice inspired our whole family with a spirit of compassion and unity.

My mother's outlook was influenced by her family as some, but not all, of her family members were very spiritual. My father was very spiritual, so when she married him she sort of increased her spiritual outlook. But my mother didn't really ever do a formal retreat or intensive spiritual practice when she was young. She did think about becoming a nun—maybe because some of her family told her, "You should become a nun, and give up all the things you have." Apparently she came from a rich family, so she had a lot of animals and other things. Sometimes relatives encouraged wealthy girls to renounce everything and go into a nunnery so they could benefit from the leftovers! But my mother did recite some of the mantras and shorter practices, such as the 21 Salutations of Tara, Guru Rinpoche short prayer, and a few other prayers of compassion. She did those practices whenever she was outside the tent working with the animals, taking care of the milk, or helping the baby animals nurse. She used those mantras all the time. I'll always remember how every single morning at dawn my mother was out milking the animals and singing the 21 Salutations of Tara. It is a beautiful memory. These are things I remember.

My father, Karma Tsultrim. He risked his life on annual trading journeys to the Chinese border in order to provide for us.

My Father's Great Hardships

My father, Karma Tsultrim, underwent great hardships and sacrifices in order to support and provide for us. Once a year, for example, he embarked on a trading journey from our village to the trading centers near the Tibet-China border, traveling by horseback or yak on an arduous two- or three-month journey. He carried with him butter, wool, lamb and yak meat, as well as yak hair that he could trade for barley, grains, rice, lentils, dried fruit, and even clothing. He loaded all his goods onto yaks, so travel could be quite slow. He often traveled through remote areas where Khampa bandits preyed on merchant caravans. He risked losing not just his goods for trade, but his very life. However, he accepted this dangerous aspect of his duty as a caregiver for his family in order to provide for us. Not in every culture or society is the father asked to undergo such risks simply to fulfill his family obligations.

A Union of Mutual Respect

My mother and father always respected each other and communicated a deep level of appreciation for each other's role. This set a proper and inspirational example for me. For instance, if my father was ever away from home at mealtime, my mother would feed all of us but not eat herself. She would wait and eat with my father, even if he didn't arrive until midnight. This isn't something she did out of fear for my father, but as a sign of deep love and respect.

My parents also showed a great deal of love, care, and understanding toward me and my siblings, and raised us with a sense of responsibility and self-discipline that has helped us throughout our lives. You might say they believed in the English phrase, "Spare the rod and spoil the child," when we misbehaved, which of course means that we were spanked occasionally. We were punished in order to understand what was wrong with what we had done. However, because my parents always communicated with loving kindness, even in these situations, the punishment didn't lead us to rebellion, but rather to increased loyalty and respect toward our parents.

The Dancing Lions

In Tibet, of course a vital part of how the family creates and teaches harmony is through exposure to the spiritual life. I remember the first time my family introduced me to a small monastery where there were 100 or so monks and nuns, probably more monks. Riwa Barmi Gon was the monastery my family was associated with, and they took me there during an annual ceremonial festival. The monks were performing spectacular mask dances and lion dances, in full ceremonial costume. That is the first time I saw such ceremonial splendor and drama as a little boy. There were hundreds of lama dances of many types—each with its own mood, style, and fascination. I remember thinking the strange creatures in the dances were real. I wondered where they had come from! The most striking creature I saw that day was a burly, bounding snow lion, who I really thought was a beautiful animal that had suddenly emerged from the mountains. I didn't want to be eaten by it, so I snuggled up very closely with my mother. Aside from the performances, I remember we received blessings and empowerments in a crowd of local Tibetan people. That was my first exposure to a monastery and lama dance, and I still remember it very clearly.

My Father's Supernatural Powers

My father, Karma Tsultrim, was a monk in his earlier years, but later gave up the monastic rules and regulations and got married. One thing he didn't, and perhaps couldn't, give up was the fact that he was a very spiritual person, doing certain practices pretty consistently throughout his life. Although I don't know that he ever did a 3-year retreat or even a month-long retreat, he did have some type of insight or realization that gave him supernatural powers. One example is that he saw things that not many people saw, such as spirits, or harmful energies, and could describe their shape and form, and so forth.

There were several such occasions I was told about, including a specific story about how he made believers out of a couple of friends. He and these two friends had been enjoying an evening at a bar in Lhasa, and as they were walking out my father saw a very strange woman standing just outside. This woman had a long bird-like beak, and as my father stared at her, transfixed in amazement, she backed away and turned. When they were outside in the street my father grabbed his friends, exclaiming, "Did you see that demoness?" His friends were baffled, "You mean that beautiful girl outside the restaurant? What are you talking about?" One thing they say in Tibetan tradition about these kinds of powers is that if the person who possesses them takes the arm of another person under his own, the other person will see what they see. So my father took the arms of both his friends under his and walked back to the restaurant where they were shocked to find that, indeed, it wasn't a beautiful girl at all, but rather the strange being my father had described.

The story doesn't end there. The next morning after my father awoke and began to go about his business out in the city he saw the demoness again; this time she was holding a very fresh heart in her hand. He didn't stick around to ask about it or anything, but he later learned that a very important person who had been at the same restaurant as my father and his friends had died that night. You could say incidents like this made believers out of the people around my father.

My father was also very good at divinations, so people would consult with him about what they were going to do, or what they needed to do about some situation in their life. Using his abilities as an oracle he would help the person make a decision. His divinations were very accurate. As a matter of fact, at least a few hundred people would all say that somewhere along the line they had gone to him to ask for his advice and he was pretty accurate. Eventually he became fairly well-known as an oracle. Being exposed to these extraordinary traits is also part of growing up in a Buddhist family.

My Uncle: "Lama in a Box"

I have an uncle, Lama Samdup, from my father's side, who did a 9-year retreat, and lived in a cabin at Riwa Barmi Gon, where I had been mesmerized by the ceremonial dances. I remember visiting him and having the feeling that he was very special, and somehow psychic. His most pronounced characteristic was that he was always very calm. My mother said that in his entire life he never once had lost his patience. And it was true—nobody I knew had ever seen him lose his patience. That was a big deal. Even then I thought it was exceptional he had never been irritated or angry in his entire life.

My strongest impression of my uncle came from the times I spent the night in his cabin, just before the communists invaded. I would peek from my bed and try to see what he was doing, because, you see, he was in a box much of the time. It was like a "Jack-in-the-box," but instead you might have called him "Lama-in-a-box!" Sometimes he would cover his face with part of his robe, but other times I could see a little bit of his face. I would watch him for a while, fascinated, and then I would sleep for a couple of hours. Whenever I woke up and took another look, he would still be there, calmly meditating in the box. He was in there day and night—basically he never slept. He was meditating all the time. I feel fortunate that I have that early image of what a real Buddhist practitioner embodies. Maybe I got some ideas about going into retreat from those scenes in his cabin that I can never forget.

My Uncle Melts Snow with his Tum-mo

In my uncle's small cabin there wasn't much room for elaborate offerings on the shrine—just 7 bowls of water and some small statues. Those water bowls stick out in my mind, because they demonstrate an interesting fact about the conditions inside his cabin: No matter whether it was summer or winter, the water evaporated very quickly. My uncle Lama Samdup was such a good meditator that his TUM-MO—his inner heat—spontaneously evaporated the moisture from his cabin.

One particularly dramatic sign of this quality happened in the middle of winter, when the snow would pile high on the roofs of the retreat cabins. These roofs were usually made of dirt or sod, prepared so that the surface was smooth and the moisture wouldn't leak through. At times up to five feet of snow could pile up there and it had to be removed so the roof wouldn't collapse. Many cabin owners had to remove this snow manually, by climbing up on the roof and shoveling it off. But some of the retreatants—the really good meditators like my uncle Lama Samdup—didn't have any snow on their roof. Instead, their roof seemed to glow with a dark red color and gently steam as if someone had built a toasty fire inside. Often they had a wet look to them, as if a light summer rain had just passed. But believe me, when you went inside, there was no fire burning. Instead, someone would be sitting silently and meditating. It sure saved a lot of work for my uncle.

Many people have witnessed this phenomenon. It didn't occur just with my uncle, of course. There were several lamas in my uncle's retreat center who had achieved this level of realization, but seeing these signs of accomplishment in my uncle definitely contributed to me becoming a Buddhist.

Licking Yogurt from a Frozen Lake

One time my mother sent me and another boy who was slightly older than me on an errand to deliver some supplies to Uncle in retreat. It was a journey of about two miles across frozen lakes and rivers, but we both loved going to see him so much that we set off with enthusiasm. We got to the point where we had to cross a frozen lake. In our load we were carrying a pot of yogurt and some KHAP-ZE, which is a whole-grain Tibetan bread cooked in butter. The way we were taught to cross a frozen lake was to throw down some dirt for traction and then walk on that so as not to slip. That is what we started to do, but then it occurred to us that it would also be fun to play around a little bit on the ice. So we were slipping and sliding around and, to make a long story short, we both fell down and the clay pot of yogurt was smashed to pieces when it fell on the ice. At that time we didn't have zip-lock bags, so there was really no way to carry the yogurt without the pot. We stared at each other, wondering what to do. Then my friend said "We'll just have to eat it because there is no way we can carry it now." He seemed to have a point, so we both knelt down and licked the yogurt off the ice, as if the frozen lake were our giant plate. I did have the scary thought that if I licked the wrong spot my tongue could get stuck on the ice and I could lose it. But as long as I just licked the part covered with yogurt it was okay, and quite tasty for that matter!

Anyway, we licked up as much yogurt as we could so it wouldn't be wasted. My friend was older than me, and he sort of took charge, directing me, "We won't tell anyone and no one will know." When the yogurt was mostly gone we hid the broken clay shards. We still had some khap-ze and probably some other things to make as an offering to my uncle, so we continued on our way.

When we finally arrived we offered him all the things that had been sent for him, except the yogurt, of course! We didn't say a thing about yogurt and my uncle seemed very happy as he spoke to both of us. He was a grown man and we were two little boys, so he was being kind of playful and smiling. He served us and chatted with us. As we ate the food he began laughing. After a while, he asked, "On your way here, did you see some little puppies licking yogurt off the ice? Did you see that?" My friend and I looked at each other in a state of amazement and guilt, and we suddenly couldn't eat another bite! We didn't know what to say! So that was the end of that conversation, but this experience had a profound effect on my childhood conception of Buddhism.

Never Steal Tea from a Psychic Lama

Another time my mother sent a Chinese tea brick to my uncle. At that time we were camped far into the nomad land, and to reach Riwa Barmi Gon would be a one- or two-day journey by horse. There were no cars, telephones, letters, mailmen, or anything that might have helped us communicate with him, but a person we knew happened to say he was going in that direction so my mother asked him to take the tea to my uncle. The man knew him as well and he agreed. He had a nice horse, and he carried with him tsampa (roasted barley), cheese, butter, and all the food he needed to eat on the way. Typical Tibetan food doesn't go bad—it is carried with the horse and you can stop just about anywhere you want to have a picnic and then ride on. You eat tsampa and cheese yourself and if you are a kind master you give food to the horse for him to enjoy. Then you have some tea and you are on your way.

The man set out to make the delivery, but it was a long journey and on the way he stopped somewhere to make tea and eat some food. Then, something happened with his mind. He thought, "This is a huge tea brick I am delivering. No one will know if I have a little bit." This man was a Khampa, a term which traditionally referred to a warrior from East Tibet. These days, you call anyone from East Tibet a Khampa, even though they aren't warriors, but a lot of the old warrior habits still thrive. For example, a lot of Khampas carry all sorts of knives, and they always have some kind of short knife for eating. So he pulled the tea out of his bag and used his short knife to open it. It turned out the tea was pretty strong, so he divided it into two equal parts and wrapped half of it up with a white scarf (KA-TAK) and the other half he put in his bag so he could try it a few more times. He figured nobody would know anything. After all, there was not a soul in sight or any contact with the outside world from where he was.

What he didn't realize was that he left the knife he had used to cut the tea brick lying there on the ground! He continued on his journey and arrived at my uncle's retreat to deliver the tea. Uncle was very thankful and happy, of course. They sat and talked and, out of gratitude, my uncle served him some food.

Now in Tibet in those days they didn't have refrigerators, so cheese was very round and very hard, and butter was also very round and very hard. Frozen meat was also hard, so really there was not much you could sit down and eat without a knife. I don't know exactly what my uncle served to this man, but inevitably he needed to use his knife. When he looked for it, it was gone. His face began to turn red, and he couldn't remember where he had lost it. Perhaps he thought it had fallen as he was riding along or something. Anyhow, he was very concerned and grew more and more agitated.

My uncle told him, "You can use my knife," and so forth but the man said, "Yeah, but my knife is a very special knife." He went on and on about how fancy it was and in despair he cried out, "Now I will never find it!"

Seeing how upset this man was about his knife, my uncle finally said, "Okay, I'll make a deal with you. I won't let anybody take your knife from where it is, and you can pick it up on the way back."

The man, of course, was quite surprised. "Where??!!" He cried.

My uncle calmly replied: "It's right where we divided the tea up." The man later related this story to many people himself, so I think he must have become a very good student of Dharma.

Doing Puja to Liberate Dead Birds

Naturally, all these marvelous experiences had a profound effect on the inner and outer directions of my life. Although I had never had any formal training in Buddhist Dharma, I often spontaneously acted in ways that made it seem as if Dharma were perfectly natural for me. I instinctually recited the melodious mantras and prayers that surrounded me, even if I didn't really understand their profound significance. But there were other more dramatic examples of how I even acted like a lama. Whenever I would come across a dead animal, such as a bird, I would place it on a rock, sit cross-legged in front of it, and conduct a ceremony in which I would help its consciousness through the bardo (intermediate state). My parents would be walking near the camp and suddenly come across me in the middle of such a ceremony—not what you'd expect of a typical boy! Later, as a formally trained lama, I learned that this is the phowa (transfer of consciousness) practice, but I did it as a child as if it were the most natural thing to do.

Though I was a typical boy in many ways, there were many unique signs in my thinking and behavior that seem to reflect a previous connection to the Dharma.

A Sparkling Landscape of Natural Entertainments

It's true we didn't have any form of modern entertainment, but the natural environment itself of the seemingly endless miles we wandered was like a giant playground full of intrigue and excitement. I remember waking up in the morning and peering out at snow mountain peaks piercing the blue sky just as the sun was rising. The white tips were transformed into majestic golden hues, reflected in the frozen lakes below. Above the mountains, slowly floating clouds projected shadows on the landscape. I stood there in the mornings, near our camp, taking in the beauty year round. In winter, everything was frozen, and the brisk air rushed past and chilled me to the bone, but as spring approached the valleys below changed to infinite shades of green, and the ice melted and flowed into running rivers and peaceful lakes. I remember walking along a lake one time and coming upon a meadow of wildflowers, so intensely hued that they colored the lake a fantastic crimson-pink. The beauty of those wildflowers remains vivid in my heart.

After hiking high into the mountains I remember looking down toward my family's tent. At early dawn, just as the sun reached the mountain peaks, which were always white with snow, it gave off a brilliant yellow color. Sometimes down below there would be a lake, often frozen, and the mountains would be reflected there.

The color of the valleys changed as the wildflowers and the seasons came and went. Colorful pasturelands and valleys were nourished throughout the summer by the crisp, melting snow. But I love this summer scene:

one side of a valley covered with white sheep, the other with black yak, and the valley below painted with the spectacular hues of the wildflowers.

Musical Mountain Medicine

We were always near a mountain, and the wind flowing around it made all kinds of subtle and unmistakable music. This music composed by the generosity of nature came to us every day, free of charge. You could hear all kinds of distinct echoes and traces in that spontaneous music, including conch, drums, and cymbals. But it wasn't a broadcast from the hall of some great monastery—it was just everyday, natural mountain music.

This auspicious wind symphony was accompanied by the gentle sing-song of flowing streams and rivers. I don't know if you can hear sounds like this anywhere else in the world. There are miles of rocks along the mountainsides, and maybe you are up there walking with friends, or perhaps going after the sheep and goats, and suddenly you hear the sound of water, but you can't find it anywhere. You listen carefully, and you can definitely hear the water, but is it just some kind of heavenly illusion? Eventually you do find the source—a stream of icy water falling from a crevice in the mountain onto solid rock. The water is rolling and running off different rocks, creating various tones and rhythms. If you follow it down you'll find it collecting into ponds and larger bodies of water.

Water in the mountains of Tibet is so clear that, quite frankly, I like it more than the bottled water you buy these days. When I visited Tsurphu recently I had a chance to drink some crystal clear mountain water, not treated, filtered, or purified by any modern devices. I couldn't stop drinking it, and I didn't get sick. A monk told me that the 3rd Karmapa, Rangjung Dorje, pointed his finger at this spot in Tsurphu and the water began to flow spontaneously. Perhaps it's due to that great blessing that I couldn't stop drinking the water.

There are also places where the water is very deep, yet so crystal clear that you can see every single stone at the bottom. You have the illusion that the stones are close to the surface. In Tibetan this phenomena is called DZA-CHU-DANG-MA: "The water that rolls on the rock." It is very pure, and good for healing. This musical, drinkable water was there in my childhood, and perhaps is still there today.

A Monstrous Bird Falls from the Sky

The yak were taken care of by a sort of Tibetan cowboy called a Khampa, and they were allowed to roam rather freely throughout the day to pasture in the valleys and along the mountainside. But those who took care of the sheep had to remain close to the flock to protect it against bears, wolves, and other wild animals. One time as my brother and I were playing in the pasture and picking wildflowers we heard an eerie sound in the sky. When we looked up, there was a monstrous bird called a TSANG (much like an eagle). It dipped toward the earth, picked up a lamb in its claws, and flew to the other side of the mountain. It all happened so fast that there was nothing we could do but hope and pray we would never have to see such a thing again. I've been told these giant birds can even pick up a young pony and carry it away.

The Vultures' Hidden Weapons Stash

Soaring way up where the rocky mountains pierced the sky you could see vultures, eagles, and other big birds soaring around in their ominous but graceful way. They had nests up there. I have been told that sometimes these great birds rob huge guns and knives from the Khampas, who often carry large, samurai-like knives.

Sometimes, when a Khampa falls asleep, his weapons disappear. The giant birds collect all these guns, rifles, and knives and they make a massive, precarious nest in the middle of a cliff where nobody can climb up or down to reach it. There is nothing for the duped Khampa to do about it. All he can do is look up and yell a few coarse words at the birds, but even if he does that, they don't seem to hear him!

Omens of Danger in the Sky

Through their deep sense of connection with the land and the living beings on it, Tibetan nomads can even tell you where the wolves are coming from, and where the wild leopards and cougars are. Even when they can't see these predators directly, they can look at the sky and tell you. Part of it is that above these hunting animals there are always opportunistic birds flying around, waiting to collect the leftovers after another animal has killed and eaten something. The crow in particular is a very interesting bird. He comes to where the sheep and goats are, and tells the shepherd (by cawing and making a racket) that there is danger coming. Then he'll fly back to the wolf or the cougar and tell him where the goat and sheep are. Very interesting. (We have a saying in Tibet that some people are like that. They cause trouble between two people by going back and forth and intentionally reporting a wrong or incomplete message.) But the point here is that when the shepherd looks at the sky and observes these mischievous birds, it is one of the ways he is taking care of the sheep and making sure they are safe. Before the wolf comes, he will definitely see some birds, and most likely a clever crow. And then he should stay close to his sheep so he can protect them. And when the wolf appears, sure enough, there are birds circling around above him, waiting patiently for leftovers. They coexist.

My Father Versus the Bear

Another fascinating animal of Tibet is the fierce and powerful Himalayan Brown Bear. When my father was a young man he went with a group of friends up into the mountains in search of one. While exploring they found a cave that might be the perfect place to find one of these huge bears. They all began to yell and scream into the mouth of the cave, but the response from deep in the dark cave was so loud and terrifying that most of my father's friends ran off immediately. However, my father had crawled up on top of the cave and was looking down into the mouth of it. When an irritated bear stepped out to explore where all the racket had come from my dad whacked him with a large stick. The infuriated bear turned and reach up toward my dad with a large, sharp claw and tore a piece of clothing from my father's body as if it were paper. You could say my dad was stuck between a rock and hard place at this point, but he displayed bravery: He smacked the bear a few more times with the stick, and as the bear was distracted, my father ran for his life!

My Run-In with the "Man-Eaters"

As it turns out, my father wasn't the only one with a knack for finding Himalayan Brown Bears. One beautiful midsummer morning I and another nomad child walked off a good distance from our tents. We were frolicking about with some lambs who had wandered that way, and not paying attention to much else.

At some point we looked up toward our camp and saw two very strange, large and hairy creatures walking towards us. Neither of us knew what they were.

"Do you know what that is?"

"I don't, do you?"

In the meantime the mystery creatures were getting closer and closer, and we awaited their arrival as if they were old friends who had come to join us. Suddenly a rifle blast exploded a large rock between us and the creatures, and the air filled with dust and smoke. The creatures were startled and ran off.

When the dust settled we looked up toward our camp again and saw that a large crowd of adults, including our mothers, were running toward us, screaming and yelling the whole way. When they got to us they hugged and comforted and consoled us. We really weren't sure what was going on until they explained that those two "creatures" had been a couple of man-eating Himalayan Brown Bears!

Ancient Methods of Reading Weather and Time

Reading the behavior of animals to tell future events is one way Tibetan people seem very close to the earth and to natural things. There are other ways they show this intimate relationship with their environment. I remember, for example, that nomad people didn't own a watch, but they could tell you exactly what time it was at any given moment. They could look up at the sky in the daytime, and tell you if it was midday, or after midday or just before midday. Sometimes they measured their own shadow. They would stand and look at the shadow, and then tell you the time quite precisely. And they could tell you just by looking at the stars in the evening what month it was—and very accurately by the way. They could also tell you whether it was going to rain or snow, just by noticing which way the wind was blowing. And they could see how sunny it would be the next day by reading the movement of the clouds. In terms of accuracy, I think the Tibetan nomads are a match for the modern weathermen and women, even without the satellites and sophisticated radars!

A Hidden Refrigerator

We were nomads and relied mainly on the animals for survival, mostly because hardly anything would grow on the harsh land at that altitude. We didn't plant and harvest crops, and the only vegetable I remember anyone cultivating was a kind of turnip. Some families planted it in their "backyards" when they were camped for the summer. It was delicious, and the only vegetable I can remember ever being grown in a garden. Mostly, we relied on the natural bounty of wild vegetables that grew at different times and places on the great plateau.

When I was growing up we did not have refrigerators so we had to store the food and vegetables we collected underground. We dug a huge hole in the ground, filled it up with meat and vegetables and covered them. When it was time to cook we opened it up, took some out, and then put the cover back on. That is how a Tibetan refrigerator works!

Roasted Rampa

Some parts of the mountains turn a striking maroon in the summer, which came from a particularly unique flower. The flower itself is white, but when the petals fall, the inside is red. We call this flower RAMPA, and it colors the whole mountainside as though it were draped in lama robes!

To collect rampa the nomads would walk along and slap the fruit with one hand into a large bag, and before long the bag would be full. After collecting the fruit they would dry it slowly, and then roast it. Then, it would be ground into a pinkish-red powder. I went to a health food store in the United States and I saw something similar—it was the right color but I'm still not sure if that particular fruit exists here or not. I'm still working on it.

The Himalayan Brown Bears have a taste for rampa too, but they aren't quite as resourceful as human beings in gathering it. During the right gathering season there are hundreds of people walking across the countryside slapping rampa into their big bags. Evidently the bears have seen this, because they've often been seen walking through the fields of rampa slapping off the fruits with their right-front paw. The problem is, they haven't figured out the part of collecting it in a bag!

Wild Mushrooms

Believe it or not, even the wild mushrooms that grew on the high plateau were beautiful. At certain times of year the mushrooms popped up for miles on pasture land where there were short grasses and no rocks and trees. They grow in large groups that form unique shapes over the grasses. And they grow overnight, as if magically—as if some intricate design has fallen from the sky and landed there in the grass. And they were so delicious. When they were young, and not completely opened, you could make a wonderful soup with them. And when they were completely open, we picked them up very care-fully, took out the root, and then cooked them over a fire. As they were cooking we'd add a little salt and butter to them, and watch their color change as the outer skin grew golden over the fire. When the butter boiled, the salt melted into the mushrooms, and we picked them out and popped them into our mouths. Once we started eating them there was no stopping. I'd say these mush-rooms were two or three times more delicious than any meat you can imagine. And at certain times of the year we could go out and pick as many as we wanted.

A Dangerous and Thorny Fruit

I also remember a delicious fruit called TAR-TOK that grew near the riverside. It grew on a thorn bush, with thorns that could really scratch you, so you had to be careful when picking tar-tok. This fruit was green when it was not ripe, green and yellowish when it was somewhat ripe, and when it was completely ripe it was yellow and red. By the time the fruit was red each bush probably had a few pounds of fruit hanging on it, and just looking at this made our mouths water! Just thinking about this fruit now, I am drooling. You put one or two pieces at a time on your tongue when you eat it, and it is different than anything I've ever tasted. It is delicious, and very hard to stop eating, but if you didn't force yourself to stop your tongue could get damaged. If you were not careful, before you knew it, the center of your tongue would be scratched and raw, and take a few days to heal.

Aside from its addictive quality, this fruit brought great beauty to the riverbanks. And it wasn't just people who enjoyed it. Many birds also loved it, particularly a type of blackbird, a little smaller than a crow, that we called CHU-WA. It had a white neck and was about the size of a pigeon. Groups of hundreds and thousands of these birds would descend on the riverside to enjoy the tar-tok.

Ruk-pa and Dza-yong: Rare, Tasty, and Valuable Treasures

Many wild fruits and vegetables growing on the Tibetan plateau are so rare and tasty they can be collected and sold very profitably. But one that the locals collected and kept for themselves was a white vegetable, long, like a stick. It is called RUK-PA in Tibetan, and grows at slightly lower elevations so it's fairly easy to find. I once saw a ruk-pa in a Western supermarket, but it wasn't quite the same. Ruk-pa is similar to an onion, but longer and all white, and it's completely edible if it's fresh. They grow in groups of 20 or 30 and we would dig them up, take off the main layers of skin, and cut up the white inside to make a soup. That's one thing I really need to find here in the West, because it's so delicious.

Another vegetable that grows high up in the rocky mountains at extreme elevations is more rare and difficult to harvest. It is called DZA-YONG. Tibetans harvest this vegetable and sell it to business people in China for lots of money. It looks like garlic, but bigger, and it is so tasty that Himalayan wild bears dig it up and eat it. Since the bears consider dza-yong a delicacy as well, you better hope one doesn't find you picking it in his territory! Dza-yong can sell for the equivalent of $500 a pound!

Dro-ma: A National Delicacy

In the lowlands of Tibet grows a vegetable called DRO-MA. Somebody told me it looks like dried potatoes, but it's not a potato. Each individual vegetable is smaller than a finger. When the leaves started to sprout on these plants, we knew it was the right time to dig them up, and some got very big underneath the ground. Once we dug them up we dried them, and they would keep for years without going bad. They were so delicious that we sometimes ate them right out of the ground, but our mouths would get full of dirt. It was a bit messy, but we enjoyed eating them like that. Of course, you could also cook them. The dried dro-ma would expand with cooking, like rice. We would add butter and tsampa and eat it like that. This is one of the finest delicacies that the Tibetan people have ever discovered, at least in the Eastern part of Tibet.

As with many tasty Tibetan treats, the people had to compete with hungry and innovative creatures to get it. In the case of dro-ma the main competition was with some little critters called ABRA—little rodent-like creatures who build elaborate underground tunnel systems. They collect dro-ma and store it in voluminous underground warehouses. Now and then a person would be digging up dro-ma the hard way—pulling the plant out of the ground like you would a potato and picking out the small fruit—when they would hit the jackpot and come across an abra storehouse fully stocked with up to five pounds of pre-picked dro-ma. That person would go home feeling like he won the lottery that day, though of course it was not such bright news for the abra.

My parents taught me another way of finding the abra's secret underground stashes. In early winter when the ground began to freeze, for some reason the ground directly above the abra storehouses didn't freeze. Someone with a keen eye could recognize this irregularity and hit the dro-ma jackpot.

Because it was such a rare and tasty delicacy, dro-ma would be saved and served only on the most important occasions, or for important relatives, family or friends who were visiting, and the dro-ma of Kham is known as the best in Tibet. It was almost comparable to serving champagne in the West. I haven't seen this one in America yet either, but I'm still working on it!

A Priceless Fruit Called Bu

By far the most valuable natural fruit of the nomad lands is the truly unique BU. It can be found in a few different places in Tibet but the best comes from Kham. It is harvested once a year—in Summer—and sold at the Tibet/China border to Chinese merchants for thousands of yuan a pound! Evidently the Chinese use bu for its medicinal properties in treating problems such as diabetes and cancer. It is also associated with longevity.

Perhaps the most marvelous thing about bu, though, is how in Winter part of the plant metamorphoses into a caterpillar, which emerges miraculously and crawls away.

A Blissful and Wondrous Childhood

Despite the difficult aspects of nomad life, these dazzling memories I describe with awe and longing are exactly how the Tibet of my childhood lives on in my heart. The unique beauty and natural wonder of our home on the roof of the world framed my boyhood experience in splendor and vastness. My family's love was my foundation as I grew and explored in the innocent, pure way a child does. Little did I know that innocence would soon be shattered by the roaring coarse of history. That dazzling world would soon slip from the grasp of my young hands. But in a great testament to the human spirit, those impermanent aspects of life, though easily erased by history, could never be erased from our hearts.

Part 2:
My Escape from Tibet to Nepal

A Moonlight Warning

One evening after dinner, the family elders were telling stories to us younger ones. Storytelling was a traditional pastime in our family, and this was the perfect night. The full moon was rising between two snowy mountains, so bright it illuminated the endless plateau for miles. Suddenly this magic moment was interrupted by the blasts of rifles, hand grenades, shouting, and screaming.

These frightening sounds started far away, but were getting closer and closer every instant. We certainly didn't know what was going on, but out of the darkness came a person galloping by on horseback screaming, "Get out, get out! We are all going to be killed! Get out now as fast as you can!" He was off like a light, but now we put the pieces together and realized the communist military was approaching. From the quality of the sounds we could guess they were as close as a half-mile away. Very clearly I remember my mother telling me to get my shoes on. Then she grabbed me by the shoulder and dragged me away. There was no time to gather anything, aside from the clothes on our backs.

Trials in the Night

Fleeing in the night, one of our first obstacles was to cross a raging river. I was too young to understand why we were escaping, and even though we were with a large group of people, the thought of getting soaked in that icy river terrified me. Yet somehow we all made it across safely and then faced our next great task: to make it up a steep mountainside. We climbed higher and higher until we finally paused to look back. In the brilliant moonlight we could see the white dots of our sleeping sheep, and the black dots of our sleeping yaks, not yet disturbed by the approaching soldiers. In front of the tents our loyal dogs were barking like mad, their keen sense of danger on full alert. At the top of the mountain we stopped once more to look back. It was nearly dawn as we looked over our sheep, our yaks, and all our earthly possessions for the last time. In the distance the sounds of rifles and bombs echoed through the sky.

We were nearly freezing and quite terrified because it was getting light, which would make us easy to find. There was nothing around us but large rocks and mountains, and certainly nothing to eat. You must remember that we were somewhere between 16,000 and 19,000 feet above sea-level. The air was thin and intensely frigid, and we had no yak-hair tents to shelter us. The older ones told us we should hide in mountain caves during the day because the military airplanes would be circling around looking for us, like vultures circling a dying animal. And indeed they did. The place we were hiding was at such a high altitude that at times the military jets were actually circling below us! I had never seen a jet in my life, and I remember thinking, "What strange noisy birds those are!"

At this point in our escape there were around 30 of us from about 7 different families, and already each family was missing some members. We hid on this mountainside for about a week. My mother had brought a few pounds of cheese with her, which together with the melted snow, kept us from starving. If we'd have gone back to the village for food we definitely would have been killed. But my dad and a few of his friends did sneak back one night and brought back some food just before we left that mountainside.

A Game of Cat and Mouse

So we moved on, but after about two weeks, as we were coming down the other side of the mountain, the military caught us. The communist interpreter told us to give up and do as they said. Of course, we were helpless, so we did do as they said. But just to frighten us and set an example, they chose a particularly old fellow from our group who was coming along on a horse, and filled both him and his horse with bullets from a terrifying machine gun. They said if we didn't listen, we would end up like him, and that we should go back where we had come from. To appease them we held our hands in the air, as if in surrender, and told them we would, but we weren't about to give up that soon, and at nightfall we continued in the same direction we had been going and managed to get away from them.

A Mirage of Unquenchable Thirst

We continued our escape, traveling by night and hiding in the mountains by day, for many weeks. By this time we had amassed a small collection of horses, so traveling was a little faster. We were trying to reach the border to Nepal or India, and as we approached we faced many hardships. Once, we went without food or water for many days. We were always on alert and always frightened. It was like a nightmare.

One night we happened upon a wide lake gleaming in the moonlight. We were all so excited that we ran to the shore, desperately ready to drink. However, one older member of our group said we shouldn't drink or it would surely be the death of us. Sure enough, the lake was a salt-water lake, whose water you could drink and drink without quenching your thirst. If you kept drinking, driven by your thirst, your body wouldn't be able to handle the salty water, and you would die. What would have been a moment of blissful relief was revealed as a mirage, so we remained thirsty.

Coral, Amber, and Turquoise Buy a Handful of Food

Sometimes we would kill a wild animal for food, but other times we carried on without eating for many days. I was weak with hunger, having never experienced it before. Often my mother carried me, but at other times I rode tied to a horse or yak.

Occasionally we were fortunate enough to come across sparse hold-outs of other Tibetan tribes. In many cases, all the men had been taken by the Chinese and only the women, children, and elderly remained. Those in my group traded whatever valuables they could find, including ornaments and jewelry of coral, amber, and turquoise right off their bodies, for a bowl of soup or a handful of whatever food was available. We had to sustain ourselves in the extreme conditions.

Stumbling Over Corpses on a Moonless Night

I remember one night we stopped to rest and cook some food. My parents told me and my brothers and sister to go collect some dry wood or yak dung to make a fire. I remember vividly what a pitch black night this was. It must have been a new moon, though the night would turn out to be very dark in other ways as well. As I went searching, I almost bumped into something bulky that I could hardly make out in the dark night. I approached it slowly, and when I was about an arm's length away I could see it was a dead man, without a head. I jumped back, terrified, and walked quickly in the opposite direction, but before long I stepped on something unex- pectedly, and nearly fell right on top of it. When I looked carefully I saw it was another dead body with a huge, bloated stomach. The outside of the corpse had a hole with blood still coming out of it.

After I got back to the group that night, I couldn't eat a bite, even though I was starving.

Crossing the Threshold of Freedom

Finally we crossed the border into Nepal and for the first time in months felt free from fear. Even though we were now refugees, we enjoyed just being alive, grateful that we had not been killed by the communist military. Tibet—that small, beautiful country where I was born—had disappeared. The escape had certainly been an unforgettable adventure, and I had learned the real value of peace and independence.

The Story of My Uncle's Passing

My uncle Lama Samdup, who had made such a beautiful impression on me with his patience, kindness, and special realizations, passed away during our chaotic crossing from Tibet to Nepal, and though I was a child, I remember his passing and its effect on me.

During the escape, his physical body was not cooperating with him, and he grew sicker and sicker. With no medical treatment available—not even traditional Tibetan treatment—he weakened, and my family knew he would die.

The night before his passing, my uncle was calm and happy. We were all gathered around him, and I remember his words: "You don't have to cry for me. I am well prepared for the separation of mind and body. All my life I have practiced meditation, and generated bodhicitta. I should cry for all of you—you need it more than I do!"

He was smiling as he spoke, and seemed completely relaxed.

My uncle died the next morning and my father, though very sad to lose his brother, had to load the body onto a yak and continue our journey to Nepal. As we crossed the border and were reaching the first village, two horsemen rode out to speak with my father. They said they were from Dopo Gonpa, a monastery of H.H. the Karmapa's that had been in Nepal for hundreds of years.

The head of Dopo Gonpa monastery, Lama Gangga Rinpoche, had sent them to pay respects to my uncle's body—very startling in a world of no telephones! They explained that Lama Gangga had a dream that a great lama had passed away, and he wanted to honor this lama. Even as a child, I recognized the special nature of the connection Lama Gangga had with my uncle, whom he had never even met.

When we arrived at Dopo Gonpa Monastery, Lama Gangga honored my uncle by coming out from retreat to show his respect. The venerable Lama Gangga and all the lamas at his monastery had amazingly long hair. Had they released it from the knots atop their heads, it would have reached the entire length of their body.

During puja for my uncle, Lama Gangga prostrated to my uncle's body—a very special and unusual show of respect, from one lama to a greater one. When the cremation was complete, and my uncle's ashes were placed in a beautiful urn, Lama Gangga asked my father to leave the ashes at the monastery, where a stupa would be built in honor of my uncle, and his ashes stored there as a relic. Later, that is exactly what they did. Lama Gangga was himself a very great lama, so his respect for my uncle was very significant.

Another highly renowned lama at Dopo Gonpa called Tsawo Lama gave my father a prediction: He said that one of his sons would become a worthy lama, while the other two sons would be successful in practical, business ways. Since my brothers are both active in the practical world, and neither are lamas, I know I am the lama referred to by Tsawo Lama. I still wonder when I will fulfill Tsawo Lama's prediction!

That year rainfall for the Dopo Gonpa monastery community was generous, and the crops were doubled. It was generally believed that my uncle's cremation was the auspicious event that caused this bountiful harvest. During our stay of many months, my family was honored as a result of this belief. Just months before, we had been on the brink of starvation, living as homeless beggars on our perilous escape from Tibet. Now, we were being treated like royalty. How quickly things can change!

Before we left the monastery, my father was offered a job managing Dopo Gonpa monastery, which showed just how much the community honored our family. He would have received a house and land for his own crops in exchange for his services. My father, however, decided to continue toward India, believing this was best for his family.

An Expatriate Tibetan Makes an Offer

During our time in Nepal my family met a Khampa man from an old Tibetan family whose name was Khampa Gepo. The man seemed lonely and insecure in his adopted country, perhaps because he was so re-moved from his family and native culture. His young Nepalese wife was childless, and the two of them wished for Khampa Gepo to adopt an heir who would care for him in his old age.

Khampa Gepo told my father he would like to adopt and raise me, and that he would give me his land and fortune if I would agree to eventually marry and raise a family in Nepal when I was old enough. He had a comfortable home, productive land, plenty to eat, and his young wife gave me treats and much attention. I think Khampa Gepo felt alienated from the local community because he was a Khampa, and meeting us had given him hope that he might find an heir from his own clan.

I was only a child, but I had suffered severe hardship during the escape from Tibet. I had lost my country, many relatives, and had sometimes been forced to beg for food and water. How good it would be to have a home, food, water, safety, and treats, too! What else could I possibly want? I told my parents I wanted to accept the man's offer, a statement that thrilled Khampa Gepo and his wife.

At this point, my mother must have realized that she would have to leave me behind when the family traveled to India, and that this would be unacceptable to her. She refused the man's offer, and said she would prefer to have her family poor and together, rather than to have a rich son who was separated from his family.

Naturally, I did not want to hurt my mother's feelings, so I agreed with her decision and my family began its journey to India.

Part 3: A New Life in India

Through the efforts of my kind father and mother, I had survived the thousand-mile journey from Tibet to India, whose unofficial promise of freedom and safety had been our goal and destination. We were now refugees, along with thousands of other escaping Tibetans, in the city of Delhi, the capital of India. When we arrived in India it was around 1959 or 1960.

Coming from the high plateau of Tibet, we were surprised by the hot weather and strange foods of India. But it was much more than just that: we were faced with dramatic cultural differences between Indian and Tibetan culture.

Strange Beings of Steel

Before arriving in India, we'd never seen a train. We'd never even seen vehicles that left tracks on dirt roads. So really those first days we had no way to relate to the large tire tracks we found on all the dirt roads, and we couldn't figure out what kind of animal had gone rambling down those roads to leave such strange prints. Of course the design was very consistent and regular, and we were wondering how the animal did that. Eventually, we saw some buses and cars and figured out what this mysterious "animal" really was.

And the train was so incredibly long, yet it moved as one long being, and carried so many people at once. Somehow we thought the train must be the mother, and the buses and other vehicles its children! We had no idea how such a thing as a train functioned. It was very hard for us to comprehend all these new technological marvels.

Food

The new foods we found in India took quite some getting used to at first. The way we ate, and the way the Indian people ate was very different. For example, they made dal (lentil soup) and a thin bread called chapatti, and all these things that didn't resemble any food we had ever seen before. But perhaps the most striking difference was just how little the Indian people ate. Their hunger was satisfied with very little food. They simply washed it down with a few glasses of water, and that was that! For some reason, we Tibetans don't really like to drink too much water. Tea, yes, and maybe a little juice, but not much water. But Indian foods had a few spices, like chili and curry, that suddenly made us want to drink water.

I remember the first time we tasted lentils with chapatti. Some Indians began giving it to us and I thought it looked a little strange. The green color was not necessarily very appetizing. I wasn't sure what it was made out of, and someone explained that it was lentils, which are generally considered horse food in Tibet! This made it even harder for me to work up an appetite for them. But I looked around and everybody else was eating, so I guessed it was okay. That was my first introduction to Indian food.

As Tibetans we had a great appetite for meat, yet when we ate the beef and water buffalo in India it didn't compare to the yak meat we had been raised on. The yak roam freely across the open plateau, nibbling on organic grasses and medicinal herbs, and this healthy lifestyle and diet affects the quality of the meat. It was another staple of nomad life we would now have to live without.

A Questionable Translator

The only language we had ever known was Tibetan, and we suddenly found ourselves unable to function fluently in India because of language barriers. And it wasn't just one language—Hindi—to deal with. We soon found out there were more than 18 different dialects of Hindi. So even if you had the fortune to learn one, it didn't necessarily help with the other 17! India was a big country with a lot of people.

This language barrier created some interesting challenges. Just after we crossed the Nepali border into India and were headed to Delhi, we found a Tibetan man already living in India who told us he knew Hindi and could get us there. Since we really had no other options, we and another Tibetan family hired him as our translator.

With his help, we boarded the train. This was my first train ride, and I was fascinated. I remember feeling like I was in a floating house. I think we were all enjoying this new experience when the Indian ticket collector started making his way through our car. We didn't have tickets. We simply didn't have any money so we had just boarded the train without them. The ticket man began speaking to us, and our translator was napping away, so we woke him and asked, "What is he saying?" He looked at the ticket man, and then at us, and said: "I don't know what he is saying...where is my bag?" We helped him find his bag, and from it he pulled out a little book, which turned out to be a Tibetan-Hindi dictionary. He paged through the book, and when he found the phrase he was looking for, he pointed to it and showed the ticket man, who smiled and nodded.

Fortunately for us, many Indians were aware of our situation, and they were quite forgiving when it came to things like not having a train ticket. It was clear our translator didn't "speak" Hindi, but at least he knew enough to help us get through that situation. Years later, after I had graduated from Sanskrit University and was fluent in Hindi, I met this translator again, and found he couldn't even say "Hello" to me in Hindi! Oh well, I am still grateful he helped my family make that first journey to Delhi.

H.H. the Dalai Lama Eases Our Path

The one phrase we could say that we knew everyone in India understood was "Dalai Lama." I guess when the Dalai Lama got to India they announced it on the radio, and in the newspapers. So all over India they read about the Dalai Lama and how he had escaped from Tibet and come to India. The government of India had agreed to help the Dalai Lama and the Tibetan government, as well as the refugees who escaped. I have heard rumors that if the Indian government hadn't agreed to help at that time, we would have been helped by the US government, or by many other governments that also wanted to help. Prime Minister Neru and the Indian people felt some responsibility for us I think, because we were their neighbors. They wanted to show us and the rest of the world that they were good neighbors, and it may have looked bad if another country had taken responsibility for our welfare during that turbulent time. So for that reason and others, the Tibetan people received a special welcome from the Indian public.

Long-Time Neighbors

Tibet and India have been neighbors for a long, long time, and there is a very strong relationship between their cultures and religions. For one thing, we share the Buddha-dharma, which originated in India. As a matter of fact, the Buddha was born in India, and his teaching spread to Tibet, China, Mongolia, and many other countries from there. So in that way, we have a strong connection. Besides that, many great Tibetan translators sacrificed their lives to learn Buddha-dharma by crossing the mountains and rivers (with no bridges and no transportation) in order to reach India and receive teachings. The journey took years, and it was all for the sake of Buddha-dharma. In Tibet there happened to be a lot of gold, so they brought that and offered it to their Indian teachers. The great Kagyu lineage holder, Marpa, took gold and went to India, sought a master, and received teachings. For 13 years and 6 months he studied with Naropa, and he said he never broke any samaya (commitment) in that time. That means he never had any doubts about the authenticity of the transmission between the teacher and himself. This is how he brought Dharma back to Tibet from India.

Impermanent Shelters

Being refugees that had just escaped from Tibet, we didn't have a tent, food, or anything of value. We were literally a bunch of beggars running for our lives. And it wasn't just a handful of us: There were tens of thousands of Tibetan refugees who were desperate for food and shelter. Everything we owned had been left behind. With nowhere to go for shelter, we often slept under the roofs of train station platforms. I must say that this was also a great teaching from a spiritual point of view. One teaching says: "All of man's creations are impermanent." Everything—all phenomena—are impermanent. You have a tent, and everything you need from your point of view, and then suddenly you have nothing. That is a great teaching, a great understanding, in some ways. I don't think everybody thinks that way, but it is a lesson I learned from this experience of sleeping as a homeless beggar in the train stations of Delhi.

My New Job

Still exhausted and hungry after our long journey, I suddenly had a new task for survival—I had to beg! This was a new experience for a boy who had run free and proud in the open mountain winds of Tibet. The great plateau had always provided everything for me and my family. Relying on the generosity of strangers for basic needs was a strange new concept, but this was the way my family and I got started on our new life. Out of generosity and understanding the Indian people did give us little things—a little change, some food, and things like that. I begged everywhere I could, collecting handfuls of change. Once, I wrapped all the change I had collected in a piece of paper before I went to sleep and the next morning somebody had stolen it! It was impermanence in the midst of impermanence! It felt like for the second time I had lost everything I possessed.

Knowing what it is like to live as a beggar is a great blessing to me. When I see people in the street all over the world, a deep compassion and empathy for them fills my heart. My experience as a beggar is like a blade that cuts away any misconceptions or judgments I might otherwise have about them. Instead, I see they are beings like me, traveling through a transitory stage of life's impermanence and blessings.

The Day it Rained Clothes

Clothing in India held a fascination for us. The Indian people dress in almost all cotton clothes, and sometimes they hardly have clothes on at all. Most of them don't even have shoes; they just walk around barefoot. And they are so skinny and bony that it was very hard for us "stocky" Tibetans to relate to them. Nonetheless, eventually the clothes we had worn on our escape from Tibet were falling apart, and we needed to replace them.

That is why I and some Tibetan friends felt such excitement one day as we were walking the streets of Delhi and noticed a huge crowd of refugees looking up to a third story window. An Indian family was throwing down clothes to the refugees in the street! My friends and I rushed to join the crowd in hopes of getting something special we could take back to our families. But only the strongest and the tallest of the refugees were able to catch the raining clothes. When the crowd dispersed and the street began to clear, we were empty-handed, and we sat down on the curb, forlorn. I began to cry.

But someone from the Indian family must have looked down and noticed these little Tibetan kids, sad and alone on the street below, because after 10 or 15 minutes someone from the house came out and tapped us on the shoulder. They invited the three of us in and served us sweet Indian tea and many delicious sweets. Best of all, they gave us some clothes. I returned to my family that day with a feeling of grateful joy. Surely the light of compassion and generosity that had warmed us that day was beyond any culture, language, country. That complete strangers could open their hearts and bless us with simple kindness gave me an immense hope that we refugees just might make it in this exotic new place.

His Holiness the 16th Karmapa. He was close to this age when I first saw him at the Black Hat ceremony in Delhi, India.

H.H. the 16th Karmapa's Black Hat Ceremony

Although our new life in Delhi was so transient and uncertain, one day we experienced a phenomenal blessing: we had the opportunity to see H.H. the 16th Karmapa. It was an auspicious occasion not only for the fact that we encountered him, but also that we were able to witness his famed Black Hat Ceremony. Of course I was still a young boy, and certainly didn't comprehend the profound significance of the occasion. I remember wondering whether H.H. the Karmapa was actually a statue. As you may know, His Holiness remains extremely still for much of the ceremony, a fact that gives credence to my memory! He sat still for so long I even remember taking a little nap. But the most powerful memory I hold of that day is how His Holiness affected the refugees and others in the audience. Even though many of us were dirt-covered beggars without even a notion of where our next meal would come from, in the glow of H.H. the Karmapa's compassionate and luminous presence, we all seemed to shine with the radiant hope and optimism of kings and queens. I believe in that moment a seed, or aspiration, was planted in me that I too would one day work for the benefit of other beings.

Hard Labor at Refugee Camp

By this point my parents and thousands of other Tibetan families were desperate for a way to maintain a livelihood in their new home. With the future of our own country uncertain at best, we had no choice but to look ahead and seek some kind of stability in India. For better or for worse, that came to us from the Indian government. They had organized a large Tibetan refugee camp in the northern Himachal Pradesh (HP) province of India. My family, along with hundreds of others, took a 3-day trip there by train and bus.

After this long journey across India we finally got to a place that actually looked a little bit like Tibet. This Himachal region is mountainous and cool, with crisp air that reminded us of the altitudes of Tibet. This is the same region where Dharamsala is located, which of course is where H.H. the Dalai Lama now lives in exile.

At the camp, the refugees' job was to build a road for the Indian government. It was arduous, backbreaking work that involved cracking the hard ground with pick-axes and shovels and clearing the land. The project we were working on was to clear away about 50 miles of rocky ground in the mountains where there was no road before. There were a few Indian people making maps and measuring, and they would lay red tags on stakes showing the way. My parents and other refugees worked 8-hour days. Men made about 3 rupees a day, and women about 2.5 rupees a day—just enough to buy food and other basic necessities. But despite the hard work and minimal pay, the Tibetans were grateful—happy to be safe and not begging for every morsel of food. Our diet was very bland and regular. Every meal consisted of either rice with lentils or chapatti bread with lentils. If we were lucky and could afford some tomato and chili it was a great luxury. We accompanied each meal with plain, salted tea with no cream, which would have been an extravagance.

The road workers were always covered with dirt, yet still always joking and laughing with one another. Remember, they didn't come home after a long day to a hot shower and a cozy bed—they returned to simple tents that the whole family shared, with no electricity. These conditions did not dampen their spirits. In the evening the young people would gather in the moonlight to sing and dance traditional Tibetan songs. The elders and we little ones would gather as well, and enjoy these spontaneous, joyful performances. This memory means a lot to me. The resilience of my people during those times is an inspiration.

Tears of Longing Outside the School Yard

The camp was located near a city called Shimla, H.P. Since we children were too young to work alongside our parents, we roamed the streets of the village during the day. There in Shimla I often passed a school with a large courtyard. When the children were outside playing, I would stop and watch them through the bars of the large gate. A deep sense of longing began to grow in my heart. I desired so badly to go to school like those children. Sometimes I wished so intensely that I could join those kids in the school that I would sit and cry as I watched them laugh and play in the echoing courtyard. For Tibetans, there was no access to school.

School Bells Ring from Dharamsala and H.H. the Dalai Lama

One day news came to the refugee camp that H.H. the Dalai Lama was opening schools for Tibetan children around India, and that he was urging parents to allow their children to attend. When I heard this, I pleaded with my parents to let me go, and they agreed to let me and my brothers make the journey to Dharamsala where the children would be sorted and assigned to a school somewhere in India. About 30 other kids from our camp had permission as well.

When I got on the bus to leave the refugee camp for Dharamsala I was full of excitement and fear. Somehow my prayers to be able to go to school had been answered. On the other hand, I was leaving my parents for the first time in my life.

Kidnapped and Bathed by a Swarm of Students

When my brothers and I arrived at Dharamsala and stepped off the bus, we must have looked like beings from another planet. From head to toe we were caked with the dust our parents and the other refugees stirred up all day building the road. Our hair was long and matted in dirty dreadlocks, and I'm sure several of us had head lice. Our clothes were ripped, filthy, and probably hanging from our bodies like thread. And here in front of us were dozens of very clean, healthy-looking kids.

To our great surprise, however, when we stepped off the bus we didn't clear the streets and attract police. Instead, a swarm of these shiny, clean kids ran up and grabbed us and dragged us directly to the bath! I was the one who ended up a bit frightened by this first impression, not them! They ripped off our dirty old clothes, scrubbed us, and redressed us in very nice second-hand clothes. They even cut our hair. For the first and last time in our lives, we said goodbye to ragged clothes, long, lice-ridden hair, and the grime that had coated every inch of our bodies.

Small Victories in the Classroom

In reality this "school" in Dharamsala was not really a school, but a center where students were to be sorted into groups and chosen for the different schools that had been created around India for Tibetan children. So I was sent to classes to begin the sorting process. I remember in my very first class, the teacher asked who could recite the Tibetan alphabet. That, I could handle! I volunteered and earned the praise of the teacher.

In another class the next day, we were asked to memorize four sentences. When the teacher asked for volunteers to demonstrate, I was again eager to show that

I could learn. The students all began to clap, and I worried that I had done something wrong—I didn't know what clapping meant! Then I realized I must have done a pretty good job because I remember the teacher saying, "You will be promoted to a higher group." Indeed, the next class I did literally move "higher." We sat on the hard floor in a room with terraced levels of concrete steps, and I was moved to the next terrace up. I still had a sore bottom from sitting on concrete all day, but to me these simple successes felt like great victories.

His Holiness the Dalai Lama. He was close to this age when he spoke to us in Dharamsala before we headed to Mount Abu Boarding School. He inspired me with the advice, "Don't waste your time!"

"Don't Waste Your Time": Words of Advice from H.H. the Dalai Lama

After some more time in Dharamsala going through the sorting classes, my brothers and I were selected, among many others, to attend Mount Abu Tibetan Boarding School. Before leaving for the school, we received a blessing and a talk from H.H. the Dalai Lama early one morning in front of his palace.

As we stood there in lines, H.H. walked back and forth, looking each and every one of us right in the eye. "Don't waste your time," he said. "Use this opportunity to study." These words from H.H. were simple enough, yet they seemed to penetrate me and take hold of something in my heart. All my life, to this day, I have taken those words of His Holiness very seriously.

Me (far right) with my brothers in our Mount Abu Boarding School uniforms. Wangdu Tsering is on the left, and Karma Chokyip is in the middle.

Climbing Mount Abu

Our journey to Mount Abu school was pleasant and well-organized. We traveled about two and a half days by train, with one stop in Delhi where they had arranged a meal and space for us to eat and relax.

Hills, jungles, camels and mango trees surrounded Mount Abu, which was in the heart of Rajistan. When the British colonists removed the King of Rajistan, his palace was put to use as a school. It housed 400 boys and girls, and many teachers and classrooms.

There is an interesting reason why the Indian government let His Holiness use this old palace as a school. During the British invasion of Rajistan there had a been a bloody battle at the palace with lots of violent killing. As a result, the palace was haunted. The local Indians could avoid it, but as students we had nowhere to hide—it was our new home! And our years at Mount Abu were plagued with many strange experiences: echoing footsteps, apparitions and sightings, and mysterious slaps on the face, even in broad daylight.

I, along with my brothers, Karma and Wangdu, and about thirty other Tibetan children, were sent to this school while our parents continued working the hard manual labor of the refugees. We were obedient and followed the strict time schedule, but I knew we each had the choice of how much effort to put into our studies. I chose to study diligently.

At first, the other children laughed at my strong Eastern Tibetan accent, so I paid another student small candies to tutor me away from it! I continued to work very hard, and after I was promoted, my classmates were nicer.

The other children played sports and games such as football and volleyball after classes, but I studied while they played. I would look for a secluded place on the playground where no one would notice me tucked away with my books, usually under a tree or behind a wall. Looking back, I guess it was a little strange that I studied so secretly, but H.H. the Dalai Lama's words always seemed to be echoing through me: "Don't waste your time!" It was during these secret study sessions that I would bribe a classmate with candies to come tutor me out of my Khampa accent.

At the beginning of my time at Mount Abu, I was at the very bottom of my class. The teacher even approached me once to say that if they had to cut any kids from that class, it would be me. That certainly motivated me! Over time, I worked my way to the middle, and even to the top of my class in some subjects. I received praise for my progress and accomplishments. During this time my Tibetan calligraphy got so good I received awards for it. I remember the teacher holding up some of my calligraphy once and saying to the class, "This is how you should write!"

By the 4th and 5th grades, I was working on 7th and 8th grade work, mainly because I studied every book before the teacher presented it. Life was peaceful—I had few worries and was able to devote myself to studying. By the time I left Mount Abu my teachers said my understanding was well above grade level. They encouraged me to keep studying.

My only other job at Mount Abu was to manage a small budget of pocket money for myself and my brothers—fifteen rupees per year. Our parents worked hard labor for twenty cents a day to give us that much, and I felt very responsible for managing it wisely. On Sundays, I took my brothers to a nearby market to buy sweets and some fried, spicy noodles called ZHI-CHAK.

Songs of Bliss Arise from Dust Clouds

Each year Mount Abu Boarding School let out for summer vacation and my brothers and I took the long trip home along with the rest of the boys from our camp to visit our parents, who soon moved to a new refugee camp in Kulu Manali, where they were busy on another road-building project. Our trip took about three or four days by train and bus.

All along the dirt road approaching the village of Kulu Manali, I anxiously watched from the bus window, hoping to find my parents among the workers lined up there. The bus stirred up clouds of dust as it roared along, and through the brown haze I could just make out the Tibetan laborers.

They really seemed more like strange aliens of dust and dirt than they did people. The features of their faces—eyes, nose, mouth, and ears—were hidden behind a thick mask of dirt. Where their clothes ended and their skin began, who could say? But there was something about these dust-smothered beings that touched me deeply. As our bus wheeled by them, nearly knocking them off the side of the narrow road, they turned to see the faces of the Tibetan children speeding by. I swear I saw smiles break across their faces, and if I listened carefully over the racket of the bus, I could hear, without doubt, songs of joy coming from their mouths. Somehow, even in that miserable and dirty state, the Tibetan refugees were happy and grateful in spirit. A great compassion and admiration arose in me for these people from my homeland. I thought of all they had left behind. I remembered the terrors of my own escape and realized that each of them had surely experienced the same, or worse.

If All Else Fails, Scream and Yell

I was always like a big brother and leader to the large group of Mount Abu students whose parents lived in the same refugee camp as mine. Once, on a trip back to Mount Abu after summer vacation, we were standing on the arrival platform at a New Delhi train station. Since there was no adult in charge, I was counting the group to make sure everyone had made it when two Indian police officers briskly approached and ordered us into their office. They asked to see our tickets, and then began to yell that we were in big trouble because we had only paid student fare, rather than the full fare, which was double. So we all pulled out our student IDs from Mount Abu to prove that we were students. But the officers still weren't satisfied, and they started to dig through our pockets for money.

This was not going well, and I had to think fast. In Tibetan, I told all my classmates to begin screaming and crying like mad until I told them to stop. That is exactly what they did! The policemen became so shocked and flustered that they begged for us to stop. "Okay, you've paid the correct fare! We'll put you on the next train. Just stop!" they pleaded. At this, I asked my classmates to stop, and the office grew immediately silent.

My Indian family.

Temporarily Blinded by the Gods

During another vacation from Mount Abu, my parents were building roads in Hamirpur, near Dharamsala, and my brothers and I joined them at the refugee camp there. An Indian family had become friendly with my parents, and during my vacation, I got to know them as well.

Mr. Rekiram Thakur owned a general store where my family shopped. His son, Kuldeep Singh Thakur, became my friend, and I got to know his beautiful wife and daughter as well. They often invited me to their family dinners and functions. In their eyes, I must have been a handsome young schoolboy, and they seemed to think I would bring their family great happiness. Apparently some of their business dealings had prospered since my arrival, and they gave me credit for this.

Mr. Rekiram's family began to give me clothes and money, and his wife gave parties in my honor. My parents were refugees compelled to live in camps and build roads for the Indian government, so the advantages Mr. Rekiram offered were exciting to all of us.

In time, Mr. Rekiram asked my parents if he could adopt me. He owned sweet shops and a cow ranch in addition to the general stores, and he said he would give me one of these shops for my livelihood. He offered gold to my parents, and took us for rides in the car to see his property.

My parents asked me what I wanted, and I replied that I wanted what was best for my family. I knew their position in the community would be improved if I were to be adopted by this Indian family. My parents then asked the advice of their lama, Venerable Nyima Rinpoche.

This high lama performed divination for my parents, and said I should not become involved with this family. My parents honored their lama's advice, and told Rekiram and his family they could not adopt me, a decision that disturbed them very much. They had hoped I would eventually marry their daughter.

On the morning that I and all the other Tibetans were to leave Hamirpur because work at that refugee camp was complete, I was getting ready to climb on to the bus when the weeping wife of Rekiram brought me traditional Indian holy objects and newly tailored clothes she had made by hand herself. She began chanting over me in some kind of ritual blessing, and then asked that I remember her until those clothes fell apart. This created quite a scene for all the Tibetan refugees on the bus: a young Indian woman creating such a fuss over a little Tibetan boy!

As I boarded the bus, a sudden sharp gust of wind tore through the inside of the bus, and I was blinded. I simply couldn't open my eyes and see. I was the only one on the bus full of Tibetans who was blinded. While the bus jolted ahead, my parents tried to help me by holding my hand and comforting me, and we were all very much disturbed.

Within the hour, Venerable Nyima Rinpoche healed my eyes by blowing on them and blessing them. When I asked him why I had been blinded, he replied that the Indian family had the protection of the local Hindu gods, and that these gods had attempted to stop my leaving. After that experience, I began to believe quite strongly that protector gods do exist.

At first, when I returned to school, I dared not write the Indian family, though they continued to write and send gifts. My friend Kuldeep Singh wrote me often and enclosed money, and in time I began writing him, so we kept a connection. They often invited me to visit, but I refused. When the daughter became ready to marry, they again wrote me, but my lama said no, do not marry into this family. In later correspondence, I learned that Kuldeep and all his brothers and sister were happily married, and I was glad for them.

I was only a young school boy when I first encountered the Thakur family, yet I received so much love and affection from them—especially Mr. Rekiram's wife. I cherish and treasure the outpouring of love I received from them, and to this day I feel blessed by it. I never did understand the reason for their special attention to me, or what made our connection so strong. Whatever the reason, I celebrate the connection and am deeply grateful for it.

Just recently I reconnected with Kuldeep through email and learned he has a successful son named Amrish Thakur. Perhaps this is a sign that our connection will remain alive for many generations to come.

Part 4: My Search for Wisdom

My Declaration of Independence

Although I worked hard at Mount Abu and enjoyed school, I eventually had to leave due to complicated family obligations, and naturally my father expected me to begin working and making some money for the family. So I returned to the refugee camp at Kulu Manali. Since I was now older and a little bigger, I worked on the roads, cracking rocks and shoveling dirt just like any adult refugee. But because I was still a boy, I got "boy's pay," which was hardly a thing. We boys working on the roads tried to get around this by wearing oversized clothes and stuffing them to look older, but it never worked.

I wanted to help my family very much, of course, but I had also loved studying and the path of knowledge. I had worked hard in school and earned good grades, and I remembered how my teachers had encouraged me to keep studying. Somehow as I pondered these things, a new realization began to grow in me: I had a choice in how my life turned out. There were many paths one could walk in this world and it was my choice whether I accepted this one or not. One day while out working on the dusty roads, something snapped in me. Very unexpectedly, I threw my pick-axe and shovel to the ground, and declared in front of everyone, including my parents, "I swear I will never touch these tools again!" I promised myself on that day that I would find another path, another way to survive aside from hard labor. To this day I have kept that promise.

A Mysterious Box from H.H. the Dalai Lama

Whatever sense of joy and contentment I had witnessed in the Tibetan laborers for many years I certainly could not capture. My small act of rebellion seemed to be part of a new vision growing in my mind that there was something of great importance for me to do. And it wasn't just my conscious mind that told me this: I also had many dreams—some very vivid and powerful. In one, I was at an enormous gathering of thousands of people. Over a loudspeaker they were calling out names, and they called mine. I didn't know why, but I heeded the call and began to walk toward the stage at the front. There, H.H. the Dalai Lama, along with other important and respected teachers, were waiting for me. When I got there, His Holiness handed me a small white box. Feeling honored and humbled, I opened it, and found many wondrously strange carved wood-block letters. They were mesmerizing and beautiful, but represented no language I knew. A voice in my ear told me "That's Sanskrit."

Deeply affected by this dream, I was compelled to seek out its mystery. What did the gathering and the graceful, ethereal letters represent? As a child I had heard of Sanskrit being a "language of the Gods," but little did I know the significance it would come to have in the future pathways of my life.

One Final Spanking

In the refugee camp at Kulu Manali there was an Indian truck driver who had begun taking advantage of his position and bullying young Tibetans. After he picked on a young Tibetan teenage boy in my circle of friends, we decided it was the last straw and that something had to be done.

We met in secret and began to scheme how we would get our revenge on the bully. These were clandestine plans with absolutely no adults involved. I suppose one of the younger boys in the group couldn't contain such an intriguing secret, because before long rumors began to spread throughout the camp of our plans.

Inevitably the rumor reached my mother's ears, who was not at all pleased with me being involved in such a lowly undertaking as revenge. When she burst into our private circle wielding a stick, everyone ran away in fright. I, however, didn't move. I sat vulnerable, prepared to face my mother obediently.

Immediately she began pounding me with the stick. Somehow, rather than pain and fear, my response was an overwhelming love and gratefulness towards her, and so I responded to each whack with a word of praise for her.

WHACK!

"I love you mother!"

WHACK!

"May you live long!"

WHACK!

"You are an excellent mother!"

It wasn't long before my mother could take no more. She dropped her stick and embraced me. We were both in tears. That was the last act of discipline my mother ever had to exert on me. My friends and I never carried out our plans for revenge. My mother and I had connected with an ancient bond of obedience between mother and child—a profound link rooted in the primordial love a mother feels for her children.

Planning My Escape

It was clear to me that swinging a pick-axe all day and smothering myself with dust and sweat was not the path to fulfill this new, growing dream of mine. I had expressed this to everyone that day on the road, including my parents. My heart was telling me to leave the refugee camp, yet I knew if I asked my family for permission to leave and strike out on my own they would never approve. My deep connection with my mother drew me to her, so one day I sat with her and told her my feelings. I told her I wished to leave the refugee camp and find something to study, or something new to do—really anything that would get me away from life in the camp. I told her I would do anything: join the army, go to school, study the Dharma. My mother, heartbroken but full of compassion, told me that she understood. Then she gave me precious advice. She told me to choose the path that would make me happy and help sentient beings, not the path that would make me lots of money.

With the secret blessing of my mother, I began to plan my escape. By auspicious coincidence an opportunity came soon after. A group of Tibetans from our camp were going on a pilgrimage to Tso Pema (The Lotus Lake), to coincide with the annual celebrations and practices related to Guru Rinpoche. I told my family I was going to accompany the pilgrims on this holy journey, and this gave me the legitimate cover I needed to leave. Once out of the camp, it wouldn't be difficult to go somewhere else instead of returning. My family happily agreed, but sent my sister, Ashi Gakyi, along with me. That would complicate my plan a little, but didn't make it impossible.

My sister and I left camp with the group of pilgrims. We journeyed by foot for much of the trip, but also took buses when possible.

Miracles at Guru Rinpoche's Lake

It was a special time of the year for pilgrimages to Tso Pema, and on this morning, thousands of pilgrims walked the concrete path around the lake singing and reciting mantras. In the center of the lake was the small, sacred island called Pay Dong.

As we circled the lake, we noticed a crowd growing in one location beside it. The sound of their chanting grew louder and louder, creating a powerful mantra. The energy created by such a large group chanting was very strong, and as the voices grew in number, the mantra became louder and louder. People had begun to toss valuable jewelry and statues into the lake, as has been the custom for 2500 years.

Then I noticed the tiny island drifting slowly from the center of the lake toward the chanting pilgrims. It was covered with tall grasses and flowers, and as the pilgrims chanted, the island moved directly toward them. It was as if it were a boat drifting toward shore, except there were no boats on the lake, and the island was a solid body of land.

We were soon able to actually touch this holy island, and to take bits of the tall grasses from its shores. The pilgrims offered ka-taks and flowers to the island, and when they had finished, the island began its slow return to its spot in the center of Tso Pema.

The holy island often moves on important dates in the lunar calendar, and on special practice days associated with Guru Rinpoche. I felt grateful to have witnessed this miracle and experienced its blessing.

A Table with Four Chairs

During the experience at Tso Pema I had a clear dream that seemed to foretell another step in my future.

In the dream I was flying on a white horse. I seemed very connected to the horse, as if it were an extension of me, and I could control it by willing it which direction to go. I flew over large open spaces, and mountains and valleys where I could see hundreds of children below. As I flew lower I could see that they were greeting me by excitedly waving scarves and handkerchiefs in the air. When I landed, they led me into a large, red building that looked a bit like a monastery, up a long staircase and through a great gate that was completely open. We entered a beautiful, ancient room. At the center was an empty table with four empty chairs. The children told me I needed to choose a chair and sit.

It wasn't until years later that I realized the total significance of this dream. Soon I would be choosing one of four "chairs"—which of the 4 schools of Buddhism to represent at university. And indeed, during my time at university, I represented my school many times, and I even remember sitting at a table with four chairs, much like the one from this dream.

Into the Unknown with a Blanket and Some Books

Near the end of the Tso Pema pilgrimage, everyone began preparing for the journey back home to camp. But the day before we were to leave, I told my sister I urgently needed to go to Dharamsala and see H.H. the Dalai Lama. I told her it was very important for me, and that she should go on home and I would return once I finished in Dharamsala. I don't think she suspected anything. We divided up what money we had left and the next day we went our separate ways. My sister headed back with the pilgrims to Kulu Manali, and I, with a handful of money, a blanket and some books, got on a bus to Dharamsala.

Rejection and Redemption in Dharamsala

When I arrived in Dharamsala I began right away to seek out the offices of the different schools and universities because I thought that might be a good place to start. Even though I hadn't been able to complete school at Mount Abu I thought if I could demonstrate my knowledge and aptitude I could get admitted to a university, since I was now the right age.

I found my way to the Office of the Education Minister for the Tibetan Government in Exile and I was fortunate to get a meeting with the Education Minister himself. He wasn't so encouraging, however. "We can't take you. Maybe you should find a job in a factory. You're a runaway, after all, and if we take you, you might run away from school too," he said.

Obviously I was disappointed, but I wasn't completely discouraged from my mission. I had come a long, long way and left everything behind, so I wasn't going to give up now. I continued to speak with the Education Minister despite his bleak advice and after he asked me a few more questions he changed his tone a little. He said I should try the Religious Affairs Office for the Tibetan Government in Exile, where all four schools of Tibetan Buddhism are represented. So that is where I headed next.

I walked into the Religious Affairs Office and asked to see the Head Secretary of Religious Affairs. I was told he wasn't in, but that I could wait. I sat and waited for quite awhile. Finally an important-looking man arrived, and the people in the office told him a young boy wanted to speak to him. He turned and invited me into his office.

"What do you need?" he asked. I told him about my history at Mt. Abu Boarding School and how I'd had to leave. I also told him how I had left the refugee camp secretly in order to seek new opportunities, especially opportunities to gain wisdom. He listened patiently, without judgment, and then asked: "So you want to study religion?"

"Sure," I said, "any way I can gain wisdom."

"In that case, you need to go to the office of the Head Representatives of the Four Schools of Tibetan Buddhism."

So I set off for yet another stop on this winding journey through Dharamsala.

I Sit Before the Four Schools

The next morning as I walked through the front door of the Office of the Head Representatives of the Four Schools of Tibetan Buddhism a tall, handsome lama was just coming down the stairs. "Where is the office of the Four Head Representatives?" I asked immediately. Smiling, he sent me upstairs and continued down the hallway.

I walked upstairs and found a room where four lamas, including the one I had just met downstairs, were sitting at a table, apparently already meeting about something. These were the four Head Representatives!

They began to ask me questions, and I answered honestly, telling them the whole story of my experience at Mt. Abu Boarding School and my running away from camp. At one point, they passed me some paper and a pen, and asked me to explain in writing why I wanted to study Buddha-dharma. I made my aspiration very clear and simple. This is what I wrote:

"I want to help myself and other sentient beings. In order to do this, I need to perfect my wisdom. Studying Buddha-dharma is an excellent way to achieve this."

Each of them took turns reading what I had written. They seemed satisfied. In fact, the next question they asked me was what lineage I preferred to study in: Gelug,

Kagyu, Sakya, or Nyingma. I told them that any lineage was okay, but that my parents had connections to the Kagyu lineage. Immediately upon hearing this, the tall lama who had met me at the door said: "You are Kagyu then. I'll take care of you." At that he stood up, took me by the hand, and led me to the kitchen, where he fed me a warm meal and we talked more about the possibilities for my future education.

Lama Lodro Tharchin Rinpoche (far right) accompanying His Holiness the 16th Karmapa (3rd from left). They had been invited to a reception by the Bhutanese ambassador.

The Lama's Auspicious Dream

This tall, sharp-looking lama who represented the Kagyu school was Lodro Tharchin Rinpoche. Of course, it was him I had first met as I entered the office, but there was much more to this story than what appeared on the surface of things. As soon as we got back to his office and I sat down to begin our interview, he started telling me about an auspicious dream he'd had the night before: He had dreamed that someone had given him the gift of a huge copper pot full of milk. In the dream he felt extremely happy with his gift, and awoke knowing the dream was about the Dharma. He had begun his day in happy expectation, looking for a sign that would direct him further.

As we were conversing, we were interrupted by the sudden appearance of a sadhu. The man was dressed only in a loin cloth, was filthy, and was interrupting an interview that was most important to me. I was patient, however, because in India these wandering holy men were respected ascetics who often possessed psychic powers.

The sadhu spoke what sounded like gibberish to me, and waved his hands in signs that were as unintelligible as his words. The Venerable Tharchin Rinpoche nodded and appeared to be listening carefully to the sadhu's words. After he departed, Rinpoche told me the sadhu had told him that I was a very special student who would complete a nine-year study of the Dharma.

Hearing the sadhu's words had reinforced Lama Tharchin's strong feeling that his dream was about me. He had known it when he saw me on the stairs, and now the sadhu had just confirmed his belief. He said I must be very significant to have appeared in his dream, and to have warranted the sadhu's visit. Then, he laughed and said, "I must take very good care of you!"

Putting action to words, he took me by the hand, arranged a haircutting ceremony for me, and offered me brand new monk's robes as clothing. I confessed that my father had forbidden me to become a monk, and that I had run away from him. My mother, alone in my family, knew my plan and approved.

At this, Venerable Tharchin Rinpoche said, "I'll take care of that. We'll take a picture of you as a monk and send it to your parents. I will explain, and they will be happy when they see you this way." That is what we did, and not long after, when I had already left Dharamsala, a happy letter from my parents arrived. Later, when Rinpoche had the picture in his hand, he said, "Just like in my dream." Then, as an expression of his faith, he held my picture to his forehead, which is a gesture of devotion normally reserved for one's teachers. He told me, "I know you are special and will succeed. Just don't forget me when I need your help."

An Auspicious Telegram

Over the next few days, while Rinpoche was working out arrangements for me to study somewhere, I worked with him as a personal secretary. Once we were sitting in his office and a telegram arrived from the Kagyu abbot of Sanskrit University. The telegram told Lama Tharchin Rinpoche that he had one available spot for a Kagyu student to enroll in the entering class of freshmen. There were ten new students from each of the four schools admitted each year. The telegram listed the first nine Kagyu students for the new class and had the tenth space blank, where Rinpoche was to fill in the name of the last student. Instead of writing it himself, Rinpoche handed me the paper and said, "Sign your name!"

So I would be attending Sanskrit University in Varanasi as an entering Kagyu student. Never in my life had I been treated with such kindness and respect. Rinpoche sent me off with a little money and a letter to the Kagyu abbot of Sanskrit University explaining my situation. I had another trip ahead of me, and I boarded the train bursting with excitement and gratitude.

Me (far left) with my brothers Karma (2nd from right), Wangdu (far right), and our friend Tsepak Dorje (2nd from left) in front of Sarnath Stupa in Varanasi.

A Solitary Moment at Deer Park

Sanskrit University is located in the Utter Pradesh region of India, which is a 32-hour journey from Dharamsala by train and bus. The hostels for the university were located in Sarnath, about seven miles from the university itself. I arrived in the middle of the night, and there was no one to be found. Sarnath is also the site of the famed Deer Park, where Buddha Shakyamuni completed the first turning of the Wheel of Dharma, so I didn't really mind having a little extra time to take in the energy of this special place. I visited the holy sites and circumambulated and did prostrations at the great stupa. (A stupa is a representation of the heart of the Buddha in monument form.) This stupa was built by the great Dharma king Ashoka. I was overcome with a deep tranquility and, in that moment, in the solitude of that holy and auspicious place, I knew in my heart of hearts that I would find success in my years at Sanskrit University.

The Kagyu student body of Sanskrit University. I am on the far left, 3rd from the bottom. (Image at bottom inserted for reference.)

I Write My Way Into Sanskrit University

Eventually the sun began to rise and I made my way to the Kagyu student hostel where dozens of young students, including the Kagyu abbot, were having some breakfast and tea. Without hesitation, I walked respectfully but directly to the abbot and handed him the letter from Tharchin Rinpoche. The abbot, whose name was Ven. Khenpo Yeshe Chodar, calmly took a moment to read the letter over. When he finished, he said, "According to this letter, you're pretty special. But we'll see about that." Immediately he ordered one of the students to bring in some chalk and a chalkboard. They put the chalk in my hand and right there on the spot asked me to write some Buddhist verses. The abbot recited the verses and I was to transcribe them onto the blackboard. Apparently, I did okay because the students in the room began to clap. There was one face in the crowd of students I recognized as a member of my clan. His name was Tsondu Seng-ge. He remembered me too, and he stood up and called out, "If he can't make it, none of us can!" The abbot, however, didn't seem so easily convinced. "We'll see," was all he said. But the important thing was that I was accepted as a Kagyu student under Khenpo's charge.

At this point in my journey I couldn't help but remember the vivid dream I'd had before leaving the refugee camp (in which H.H. the Dalai Lama had given me the box of Sanskrit letters) and reflect on the obvious and profound connection it had to my current situation at Sanskrit University.

Students from all four schools of Tibetan Buddhism in my class at Sanskrit University. I am seated in the first row, 4th from the left. (Image at bottom inserted for reference.)

A Simple Life of Learning

I immediately began to study Sanskrit, Hindi and Buddhist philosophy. These were challenging subjects that required serious focus, and I quickly adjusted to a life of minimal comforts and distractions in which the greatest excitements were the fruits of knowledge and wisdom that came from diligence. We woke at 4 a.m., with only the white stars of dawn to greet us as we walked out to catch the bus that would transport us from the hostel where we slept to the university itself. If you happened to miss the bus it was a long hike and even with great effort you weren't likely to make it to class that day. But at least in these early hours the oppressive daytime heat was not yet upon us. The Indian sun cooked the earth like an oven. There was no air conditioning, and I think I could have cooked my meals on the hot ground had I wanted to. Even at night the air was thick and humid. It was so hot I slept on the hostel's roof in the open air, lying safely under a mosquito net. Mosquitoes buzzed and sang all night, anxious to sample me for a midnight snack.

I lived on about 50 rupees a month, which I received through a scholarship offered by the Indian government. In order to continually qualify for this scholarship, I had to pass all exams twice a year. At that time, 50 rupees was equivalent to about 3 dollars. I had no choice but to create a life of few unnecessary expenses, and I did manage to live 9 years on that modest stipend.

An Embodiment of Wisdom

In my years at Sanskrit University I met many learned lamas and teachers who blessed me with their patience, compassion, and wisdom. But Geshe Yeshe Thubten inspired me especially for his remarkable embodiment of wisdom. A small group of us took a private class with him on Abhidharma, or Buddhist metaphysics. His ability to read a text and immediately identify its "root," or origin, and essence astounded me. It was as though his mind were a great temple where Dharma texts were neatly arranged on shelves. At will, he could describe the location and relationship of any of these texts to one another.

Geshe Yeshe Thubten did a lot of Milarepa practice, and he kept a book of Milarepa's songs under his pillow as he slept. He had a deep connection to the Kagyu lineage, yet he was very open and non-sectarian. In fact, he was often surrounded by people from all four schools, who came to benefit from his wisdom and qualities. I remember once a group of students from all the schools were gathered around him. He was singing Milarepa songs, and was overcome by such devotion that he became emotional. This, to me, was a sign that Geshe Thubten's Dharma came from the heart and was motivated by bodhicitta for all sentient beings. His non-sectarianism, sharp mind and open heart were a vital inspiration to me.

My dear friend and father-figure, Jean Claude.
With his support I made it through some very difficult times
at Sanskrit University.

I Find a Father in Deer Park

I attended classes all morning and then took lunch with my classmates. After lunch, I would take a nice long nap—under a mosquito net, of course. After this "power nap," as it might be called today, I studied hard well into the evening. On these long afternoons I had a favorite spot under a tree in Deer Park, where I would sit with my books and meditate and study.

The open parkland was the site of the Ashoka Stupa and many other Buddhist monuments and temples. It is where Buddha is said to have first turned the wheel of Dharma. Peacocks and deer would stroll about, and one could find relief from the sun by sitting under the trees.

One afternoon I sat in the shade of the huge, sprawling tree where I liked to sit and chant Buddhist texts. I noticed some Western tourists visiting the stupa, and was happy when one of them, an older man, approached and asked if he might speak with me. I invited him closer, and offered him my meditation cushion.

The gentleman, who I learned was named Jean Claude, was tall and thin and he leaned upon a silvery cane. Though he was French, we spoke in English. My English was very limited, so we also used a lot of hand gestures. He asked me many questions about what I was studying. He also wanted to know more about Sanskrit, Buddhism and Tibet and its losses.

Jean Claude asked me to show him around the park, and tell him about the stupa and temples, which I was happy to do. Afterwards, we had a cup of chai (tea) from a teacart vendor across from the stupa. We sat on a bench and exchanged addresses.

A few months later we began a correspondence, and within the year, Jean Claude returned for the first of several visits he made over the next few years. We met at the same place each time and had many pleasant conversations. He brought me gifts, and I gave him small Dharma gifts in return.

Over the years he visited my parents with me and told me about his two daughters. At one point years after we had met he asked to adopt me and take me to Europe, but my parents refused, though we all appreciated his support and kindness. Over the years, I have maintained correspondence with Jean Claude's daughters, and I remain grateful for his friendship and support.

A Mysterious Invitation from H.H. the 16th Karmapa

One day during my time at Sanskrit University H.H. the 16th Karmapa was passing through nearby Varanasi on a pilgrimage of holy sites. Since he was so close, he stopped to offer blessings to the students of Sanskrit University. This was big news to the community around Varanasi and there was a huge gathering of people that was alive with excitement and anticipation.

I got in line with the few spare rupees I had and a ka-tak offering scarf. His Holiness was giving the blessings from his car and the long line of students filed past one by one. As my turn came, I approached with a reverent bow and made my offering, and was astounded when His Holiness gestured for me to step closer to him. When I did, His Holiness spoke to me: "Come up."

All I could do was nod my head in agreement. In fact, I wasn't certain that I hadn't just imagined it. As I stepped away I sort of stood to the side and watched the other students approach. I wanted to see if His Holiness was speaking to everyone. But I watched as one, two, three, four, and more students passed by, and His Holiness didn't utter a word to any of them. What did it mean? When I later mentioned it to some close friends they told me that it surely meant I should go to His Holiness' monastery in the mountains of Sikkim which, after all, was "up" in the mountains. I was intrigued, but Varanasi was far away from Sikkim, and I was so busy and focused on my university studies. It didn't seem like the right moment to act on it, so I just let the invitation rest in the back of my mind.

My beautiful sister, Ashi Gakyi (right).
Without her help at home, my brothers and I would never have been able to attend school.

Penpa Tsering and Tsomo's family.

A Role in My Sister's Marriage

During the years that I spent at Sanskrit University I got news from my family that my dear sister Ashi Gakyi was going to be married, and they wanted my advice and approval in the matter. I was the eldest son, and the trust my family placed in me as an advisor gave me an opportunity for growth and increased responsibility.

Ashi Gakyi had worked hard in her life, cooking and laboring to help our family survive the difficult years in the refugee camp. Our whole family depended on her—my younger brothers in particular. After all, my brothers and I had gone off to school while she stayed behind and cared for my parents. In a way, she was the one that made it possible for us to get an education. No one in our family wanted her to marry and move away, but we knew it was time, and we wanted to help her make a good marriage.

A gentleman named Menlha had put forward his nephew, Samdup Tsering, as a suitor. The two men were on leave from the Army, and young Samdup Tsering was very handsome, well-dressed, well off, and, frankly, irresistible to a young available lady. They had spoken to my sister directly, and she had answered that she would do as her family wished. My parents consulted me, and I agreed to the marriage.

We were so poor that a traditional Tibetan wedding was out of the question. Instead, our small group gathered in front of a shrine to celebrate the marriage of Ashi Gakyi. Even now, I feel responsible for my sister because of the trust she placed in our family's judgment.

This responsibility I feel is especially poignant because I can remember teasing her when we were very little. Once, I pushed her into a pile of yak dung, and she cried that her hands were dirty and she called me mean. She was so young she did not know the dung could be washed off, or that yak dung is actually very fresh smelling! To this day she has not let me forget that episode!

My brother Karma's family.

My Little Brothers Grow Up

One beautiful thing about my connection with my brothers is that I don't ever remember beating them up, though I do remember fighting in order to protect them. Just as my sister had grown up and continued her adult life by marrying, my brothers were growing up as well.

My youngest brother, Wangdu, has always worked very hard at whatever he does, and always with selfless motivation. His main focus is always to support others—our parents, his own family, and he even gave me a lot of financial support when I was studying at university. It is true that Wangdu finds himself in trouble sometimes due to his colorful personality, but I believe his heart is in the right place, in that he especially cares for his loved ones.

Neither of my brothers could attend university because of their own family and financial obligations. However, that especially did not keep my middle brother Karma from being successful. He is a very good and respected man who embodies many of the greatest human qualities. He has worked hard and honestly for his community in South India and has earned so much respect that he was promoted to a position in which he manages the finances for the entire community of 10,000 to 15,000 people.

I sincerely believe that without the help of my dear brothers I wouldn't have been able to complete my university studies. Out of gratitude I try to give back to them everything I can. Today, they both have healthy, beautiful families and our relationship remains strong and positive.

Who is King of the Jungle?

My parents lived and worked at the refugee camp at Kulu Manali for many years, but during the time I was at university they found out that the Indian government was leasing some land to Tibetan refugees in southern India. To my parents, it seemed like a good opportunity to move on and gain some independence, so they packed up all their possessions and again headed for a new home.

I happened to be home visiting during this time, so I accompanied my parents on the four-day journey. We took buses and trains, and both were jam-packed with other Tibetan refugees and all their imaginable possessions.

When we arrived at the new land, we all built temporary grass and bamboo huts to live in while we got settled. This new environment was even more of a contrast to Tibet than Northern India was. It was a dense jungle, full of lions, tigers, elephants, monkeys, pythons, and wild boars. Our most immediate concern, though, was that our simple huts were not good at keeping out the very resourceful rats who came searching for food. We would hang our food in bags up in trees so as not to attract so many, but I still remember being kept awake at night by these giant jungle rats coming into the hut and nibbling on my face and toes. My simple life at the university seemed like the lap of luxury compared to our experience in this new jungle. At least back at school there was nothing bigger than a mosquito out to eat me!

Tibetan families like mine leased pieces of this land so they could grow crops, which was no simple endeavor. First, big bulldozers had to clear away portions of the jungle. Once this was done, the earth below was quite tough. And to top it off, Tibetans were experts at raising yak and sheep, but none had ever grown a crop before. Corn can be quite stubborn—even compared to yaks! The refugees had to learn to farm. Of course their great ability to adapt would once again prove to be key to their survival.

Now, once the corn finally began to grow, the people weren't the only ones interested in it. Wild elephants stomped through the fields looking for something to eat, and if 20 or 30 elephants destroyed your crop, you were done for that year. But there was one way to keep the elephants out: dig a deep ditch all the way around the settlement. The elephants were afraid to cross it, so it served as a reliable defense against them, but not against monkeys and boars, who were another story altogether.

By the next time I came to visit my parents, they had begun to establish a new way of life at this new settlement, and they had even built a permanent brick home on their land. That visit I slept much more soundly!

Final Exams

At the end of my undergraduate years, the ever-important final exams loomed. I, like all my classmates, wanted to continue studying after I completed my Bachelor's degree, and go on to graduate school. Before that could happen, though, I needed to qualify by passing the final exams. Even though I didn't believe I was the smartest in my class, I promised myself I would work harder than ever, and studied many hours. Often I would study all through the night, stopping only when the morning gong rang to begin the next day.

On exam day the tension was palpable—there was so much riding on it for all of us. One of my classmates was so nervous he was having trouble reading his exam. It seemed he suddenly couldn't read Tibetan anymore, until he realized he had his test upside down! I fulfilled my promise to myself by giving a complete and sincere effort on the exams. Throughout my years of study I had never cheated, and always let my effort earn what it may. Now, there was nothing left to do but wait for the results.

Holding Our Breath for the Top 15

At this same time, near the end of my undergraduate years, Sanskrit University began to experience some financial turmoil. Many scholarships, including mine, were in danger of being lost. School administrators consulted H.H. the Dalai Lama and Indian officials for a solution to the crisis. In the meantime, many of us protested in hopes that we could prevent our scholarships from being eliminated. This period of limbo lasted about six months, during which time our stipends were suspended.

Of course the stipend was my only source of income, so I certainly never would have survived those six months without some outside help. I wrote to my second father, Jean Claude, explaining my predicament. Without any hesitation he simple asked, "How much do you need?" He became my sponsor and adopted me as if I were his own son. Through his generosity I was able to weather that shaky period at the university, and I have always been deeply grateful for that.

Finally, at the end of this long period of doubt, school administrators called us into an assembly to announce the solution that had been reached by the Indian Education Minister and the office of H.H. the Dalai Lama. It was official: There was not enough funding for everyone to continue their graduate studies. Only 15 students out the 40 in my class would continue to be supported, and they would choose the 15 by looking at the scores on the undergraduate final exams. Now, we had heard rumors that everyone had passed their exams, but where we each ranked in the scoring, we had no idea. The assembly—which was attended by the whole student body—was shrouded in anxiety. No one dared to breathe until the names were called. These 40 students represented all four schools of Tibetan Buddhism. Those who didn't make the top 15 would not be able to continue their studies unless they could somehow support themselves, and for me it would certainly mean returning to my parents in South India and a life of hard labor.

One by one they called out the names in order of the top fifteen, and the identified students stood up. The ninth name that echoed through the assembly was mine, and I stood up full of relief and joy. I had studied extremely hard to prepare for the exams, but some of my classmates who I knew were more learned than I in certain subjects didn't make the top 15. These were people who I had asked for help on certain subjects. I prayed they would find a way to continue their education and find the means for their dreams and aspirations to be fulfilled.

Courage Under Fire

Over the next 3 years I worked toward my Archarya degree, the equivalent to a Master's degree in the West. At this level there was much less focus on language study and more deep study of Buddhist psychology. In frequent intense, all-night debates we were expected to defend fine philosophical points and demonstrate our knowledge of important texts.

There were short debates almost every evening with our classmates, but a few times a year there were more intense debates in which the whole student body of the individual sect participated. So in my case, for example, I participated along with every other Kagyu student at the University, of all years and levels. Now we were studying the deeper and more complex texts of Madyamika (the Middle Way), including the texts of Nagarjuna and Chandrakirti. In these all-night debates two Archarya students were selected and seated on cushions facing the rest of the Kagyu student body. There were teachers sitting to the side to moderate and evaluate the debaters' responses. I remember sitting there myself as one of the selected debaters, sweating profusely. The tea I was sipping didn't have much taste, and the room seemed extremely hot.

The two of us took turns answering questions put up by our fellow students. Because we were ninth year students, we were responsible for anything we had learned in those nine years! I remember we answered most of the questions, and as the night went on the room got cooler and the tea seemed to taste better. In some ways this was a very serious event—We were demonstrating our knowledge and wisdom publicly to the whole Kagyu student body (30 or 40 students). I can't say I answered everything perfectly, but overall I'd say I performed above average.

Not for the Weak-Kneed

Aside from the regular debates within each school there was an annual debate that was very important because it pitted Archarya classes from two different schools against each other in a debate of subtle points of Buddhist philosophy. In one of these debates, my Kagyu class was set to debate our Gelug classmates. H.H. the Dalai Lama was going to attend, so there was a lot of anticipation.

On the day of the debate the hall was packed with hundreds of monks and esteemed lamas, not to mention H.H. the Dalai Lama and his entourage! The Kagyu class was seated on the right, and the Gelug class on the left. They would choose the debaters from each class by drawing names, and I was sure my turn was up. I hadn't been chosen yet and I had a feeling it would be me. Instead, though, one of my classmates was selected. I'm not sure if I felt disappointment or relief, but as for my classmate—I know he was very nervous.

Before the actual debate we all drank tea in an intense silence in which the only sound was the occasional clinking of a tea cup. Finally, it came time to debate. As my classmate stood, his legs were shaking, and when the debate began, he paced back and forth. He was so nervous he wasn't paying much attention to where he was walking, and we had to frantically lift the tea cups from the floor as he passed so he wouldn't trip or send them flying everywhere.

The two debaters were both so anxious to get their own questions out that they began asking each other questions at the same time. Of course this didn't make for a very interesting debate, and I noticed H.H. smiling at this situation, and the whole audience began to stir. Finally, the Gelug debater relented and answered my classmate's question. The debate began.

After three years of study, with great fortune, focus, and hard work I graduated from Sanskrit University with a distinguished Arharya degree.

Receiving my degree from the Indian Education Minister.

Me with my retreat master, the Very Venerable Kalu Rinpoche.

Part 5:
Seclusion and Empowerment

"I Can't Get No Satisfaction..." (in Samsara)

After my class had graduated we were gathered in an assembly of the Kagyu student body and they read-aloud a letter from H.H. the 16th Karmapa's General Secretary. The letter described an open position in one of His Holiness' publishing projects—they needed a very learned editor/proofreader. Without hesitation I raised my hand and accepted the position. I thought to myself, "I can't think of a better job than helping His Holiness through his publishing projects."

I traveled from Varanasi to Delhi, where the position was located. I was the chief managing editor for a project to publish the KAN-GYUR—the entire collection of the Buddha Shakyamuni's teachings. It was a good job with very good pay. I was living comfortably and, truth be told, I couldn't have imagined an easier lifestyle. Many lamas were working on the actual transcriptions, and I was simply responsible for the final proofread: If I thought it was good, I would give it my stamp of approval. My new role brought good money, high respect and honestly, many of my classmates from university would have considered it a dream job.

Yet somehow, even with this fortunate position I was still unsatisfied. Delhi is the capital city of India and an international center of business and trade. It is busy with the comings and goings of people from all over the world, and I began to see that life there was full of distractions. I wondered what all the knowledge and wisdom I'd gained from academic study was good for if I was here in the bustling city, just as distracted as any other resident. I began to feel that now was the time to practice in a seclusive retreat, and experience for myself the realizations of Dharma that come through intensive practice.

I wrote letters to two retreat masters: Venerable Bokar Rinpoche, and Venerable Beru Khyentse Rinpoche, explaining my situation and asking if they would accept me in their retreats. I told myself I would focus on the one that responded first. I knew, in fact, that both retreats were under the guidance of the very Venerable Kalu Rinpoche, so I had complete faith that either one would be blessed by his enlightened wisdom and activity. They both responded quickly, saying they would be happy to have someone with my level of education and experience enter their retreat. However, Beru Khyentse Rinpoche's letter arrived first, so that is the invitation I accepted.

In my job I reported directly to H.H. the 16th Karmapa's publishing manager, Tsongpon Konchok. Now I had to approach him to tell him I wished to leave my position. At first I didn't explain I was going on retreat, and he got very angry. "What good is your degree," he asked me, "if you can't help the lineage?" He even offered to increase my salary to entice me to stay. I finally had to explain that money wasn't the problem—I wanted to enter retreat. But he simply didn't believe me, and still wasn't prepared to grant me permission to leave. "Look," I said, "Time will tell us who is right. If I do nothing but go straight to retreat, then I am right. If I go do something else, then you are right. Time will tell." He responded with silence, but finally let me go.

Years later, after I had completed retreat, I went to visit him. Happily, there were no hard feelings lingering between us. He was happy to see me, and took me out to eat at a restaurant, where we chatted and laughed about it.

An Auspicious Coincidence

On my way to enter retreat with Beru Khyentse Rinpoche I enjoyed some very happy and auspicious events. I was traveling from Delhi to India's Bihar Province, not too far from Bodhgaya. When I arrived at the small city of Ambikapur, which is still a couple hours by bus from the retreat camp at Mainpat, I learned I would have to wait until the next morning for the bus to take me the final leg of the trip. At the hotel, I met a friendly young couple who was also traveling to Mainpat in the morning. As we were getting along well, we looked forward to making the bus trip together. To me, it felt good to have some friendly traveling companions.

When I spoke a little more about why I was headed to Mainpat, the young woman further delighted me by telling me her father, the very respected head leader of the camp, had spoken of a young monk he was expecting at the retreat camp. He was, of course, referring to me! Her father's name was King Namkhai Dorje, and I felt honored he had mentioned my arrival.

As we arrived at Mainpat a large gathering of people was forming, and the manager of the monastery greeted me and took me into the kitchen for tea. As I sipped, he told me my arrival was fortunately timed, and I appeared to have auspicious connections. That said, he urged me to drink my tea quickly and proceed directly to the shrine room. He explained that Ven. Beru Khyentse Rinpoche had just returned from abroad and he was about to begin a longevity ceremony in which he would make special offerings. It seemed I was indeed arriving at a special time!

Just as a monk escorted me into the shrine room, Ven. Beru Khyentse Rinpoche was beginning the Mandala Offering Ceremony before a crowd of hundreds of monks and lay people. As part of the ceremony, Rinpoche gave an exceptional and unprecedented gift to each of the monks—a cash gift of fifty rupees each. It didn't necessarily mean much in terms of dollars, but such cash offerings are rarely heard of and it was very unusual that Rinpoche would give such a gift at all.

As the ceremony ended, I was welcomed warmly by everyone. The local people called out that "the new lama" must be a very special being to arrive at the precise moment of the longevity ceremony. Their words flattered me, though I really did not believe I was such a special being! This was, however, an auspicious coincidence and a very joyous beginning to what would be the 3 most transformative years of my life.

Me (far left) with my three-year retreat mates. I was inspired and motivated by these heart-felt practitioners. In center of photo: Retreat master Venerable Lama Dodhy Rinpoche.

While in retreat, my hair grew long—
hopefully along with my wisdom!

My Hair Grows Long

I entered retreat under Ven. Beru Khyentse Rinpoche at his retreat center near Bihar, India, about one day's journey from Bodhgaya. In retreat, of course, you concentrate all your time and energy without exception on purifying your obscurations—on clearing away or cutting through whatever is keeping you from recognizing your true nature. There was intense meditation and study all day, and even at night we engaged in dream yoga practice, so really not a moment was wasted. A student once asked if, when I was in retreat, I was ever worried I wasn't getting enough sleep. My answer was, "On the contrary!" I was more worried about not wasting even a single minute of that precious opportunity for practice.

Certainly retreat can seem lonely from the outside. You spend nearly 24 hours a day in your cabin. And even within your cabin, most of your time is spent inside your "box." The only people you see are other retreatants and the cooks, who are your only contact whatsoever with the outside world. There are obviously no phones, TVs, restaurants, bills to pay, friends to gossip with, or leaky roofs to fix. With these distractions gone, the only thing left to face is the greatest and really only true obstacle of all: your own mind.

Early in my retreat I experienced great difficulty. There was a very strict and structured schedule of group and individual practices, as well as many new texts and practices to learn. I struggled with my physical body a bit—my knees and legs hurt from sitting cross-legged so much. Eventually, though, my body adjusted and began to deeply relax. As my body relaxed and as worldly distractions faded, retreat began to feel like a great rest after a long, tiring struggle. Though I hardly left my tiny cabin, I had many wondrous experiences that 100 journeys around the world could never have matched. Away from the demands of the mundane world, my hair grew and grew, as perhaps did my wisdom and insight. This I do know: if I hadn't entered retreat I certainly wouldn't be the gentle, jolly person people claim I am today. That intensive practice deepened my patience and purified my negative emotions in a way I never would have understood before retreat.

I Learn of My Father's Passing

Despite the fact that we had no modern communication technology, it seems there are other ways to communicate with fellow beings. One night I dreamt of my father dressed in very different clothing than he would normally wear. My heart told me he was dressed that way because he would be leaving: He was dying.

I immediately wrote a letter to him—I sent it with the cook—urging him to do practice to increase his longevity and health. But it arrived too late—my father passed away three days before it got there and there wasn't much I could do. Because of the tight restrictions I could not leave retreat, so I engaged in extra practice on his behalf, hoping the blessings would reach him in his transition. I thought back to the last time I had parted with my parents in South India. At that goodbye, my father had seemed irritated and emotional—very unusual for him. I now realized that even then I had known it would be the last time I would see him.

At this time I also began to understand that these powerful dreams of mine were very accurate, and always came true. After 49 days of practice on my father's behalf, I had another dream which I took as a sign that he was doing well. In the dream he was young, happy and dressed very nicely. The sight of him was so realistic that I had to remind myself it was just a dream.

My father's legacy to me are the profound lessons he left me throughout his life. He showed me one should never give up in the face of challenge. You should be tough, yet never take advantage of those weaker than you: Show compassion.

There are a few stories I heard later about my father's passing that add to his memory. Right after he died, two well known lamas from two different Tibetan Buddhist schools were invited to attend to his body before his cremation ceremony—a traditional custom. Both Venerable Tana Tulku and Venerable Khamtrul Rinpoche agreed my father's body showed signs of realization. "Did he do retreat?" they both asked. He hadn't done any retreat that anyone knew of, but both lamas agreed he wasn't an ordinary person in terms of realization. Spiritually, he was well prepared for death. Much of my family was shocked and surprised at this news, but for me it simply confirmed the messages in my dream that he had made the transition through the bardo well.

My mother told me another story. Less than three days before his death he woke up in the middle of the night and went to the kitchen and prepared a meal. My mother, of course, wondered what was going on, but my father was calm and happy. He spoke with my mother about impermanence and reassured her that she would be okay. It certainly seems he had a premonition about his own death, and I take this as another indication of his achievement.

So it happened that my father passed while I was thousands of miles away in retreat. In the mundane view, you could say this was a bad thing: I couldn't be there to help him and comfort family. But from a spiritual point of view you could say I was blessed to be in a powerful retreat when it happened. After all, I was able to see my father's progression and, in a way, communicate with him even though I was far away and "incommunicado." Because all beings are interconnected, these telepathic ways of communicating with one another are possible.

Our Retreat Cook is Attacked By a Naked Zombie

Believe it or not, retreat is not totally free of comedy and drama. Our cook was a gentle, very attentive man in his sixties. He did a great job caring for retreatants, and he never let us down. He often made the journey from the retreat to the village market for supplies, and on these little trips into the village he frequently enjoyed a beer or two. This didn't affect the quality of his meals or anything, but later it would come back to haunt him!

To end our day of practice, at about 10 p.m. or so the 12 lamas in retreat did Chöd practice together. There was one lama, though, who was excluded from this nightly practice because he was hard of hearing and the playing of our bells and damarus (drums) had to be coordinated in perfect synchronicity. Since it was dark by that time, it would be hard for this lama to participate, so instead the retreat master gave him a personal practice to do in his cabin.

Well, one night while we were doing Chöd practice, this lama stepped out of his cabin to go to the bathroom. Since our retreat was very isolated and it was dark, he stepped out without his robes on and walked gingerly in the moonlight outside the gate. In other words, he was completely naked.

Now, at the same time, the cook happened to come out with the intention of closing the gate for the night. As he approached, what should he find coming toward the gate from the outside, but a naked figure. You have to understand that there were already many strange things happening, and that the retreat center was very near a cemetery. These things must have been on the cook's mind when he saw this figure, because he went hurrying toward the gate to close it and keep this zombie out.

The lama noticed the cook was about to close the gate, and of course he was worried about getting locked out for the night. So he went running toward it as well. Since this lama had taken a vow of silence, he couldn't really talk, so he began to sort of grunt loudly at the cook, which didn't calm the situation at all! When they both reached the gate, the cook was closing it, and the lama reached through the bars with a desperate look on his face and grabbed the cook's arm. The poor cook, who'd already had a couple of drinks that day, could take no more, and he passed out. The lama could do nothing but return to his cabin, but when the cook woke up the next morning he thought he had been attacked by a naked zombie! Unfortunately, because this lama had taken a vow of silence, it was some time before the matter could be cleared up and the rest of us could enjoy the story.

Sharp Claws In My Back

Not all strange occurrences during retreat were explainable by such conventional means. One late night during Chöd practice I felt sharp claws dig into my back. You have to remember, we had no electricity and it was completely dark. I couldn't simply turn around and see what was there. It was painful, but I didn't want to drop my bell and damaru, so I just ignored it, thinking maybe it was just my mind, anyway. Besides, our retreat master Lama Dodhy had warned us several times that during these intense practices—especially Chöd, in which we are literally offering ourselves as a meal to sentient beings—we might have the experience of being chased or attacked. Finally, the claws released. Later, during a part of the practice that involves silent meditation, I heard a cat's meow and looked over to see a cat at the doorway. I figured that was the explanation, but I decided to tell the retreat master the next day anyway.

"Maybe it was a cat for you," he said, "but that's not what it really was!" It seems someone had been testing my practice.

Fighting a Snow Leopard

I had another experience with a feline, although this one was much larger and came to me in a dream. I remember it vividly even now.

I was hiking in high snow covered mountains, and a little crystalline river was streaming down the mountain, splashing musically. It was full of stones, and in the center of the river, stones were protruding out of the water and their tops were covered with such perfectly undisturbed snow that they looked like white mushrooms. As I walked higher into these beautiful mountains, I felt as secure and comfortable as if I were with several good friends.

I began to notice huge, non-human footprints, and suddenly there was a powerful noise and the earth seemed to shake. Out of nowhere, a snow leopard materialized and was on top of me. As he was fiercely attacking me, I had no choice but to fight back. We wrestled back and forth in a tangled struggle, rolling over and over on the ground.

Suddenly, I felt great confidence and strength, and I was completely unafraid. With two strong hands I reached into the leopard's mouth, placed one hand on each jaw and pried it open with such strength that his head split into two parts, which I tossed aside.

I felt so proud to have vanquished the powerful leopard that had attacked me. Yet, I also felt sad to have killed another creature, and I turned back to give one last look at the once fierce and regal leopard. To my amazement, where I had defeated the leopard lay only a dead cat—about the size of a house cat. I could not explain what had happened, but my pride was immediately deflated.

Flying a White Horse

During retreat I had many vivid and auspicious dreams, and one was especially magical and meaningful for me. In it I was on a powerful white horse that flew through the sky. We crossed over deserts, forests, plains, valleys and mountains. In each of these places I looked down and saw thousands of people of many different colors shouting for water as though they were suffering from a terrible thirst. Indeed, as I flew lower I noticed the land was parched and dry, and these people were in fact desperately thirsty children. As I flew by the suffering crowds I said, "What do you mean? There is water there, and there, and there..." Each time I said "there" I pointed to another spot in the landscape, and a geyser or stream of sparkling water began to shoot up or flow from the ground. The children clapped their hands and cheered as they joyfully ran for the water to relieve their thirst. I continued on to more and more lands, using my miraculous power to bring relief to as many beings as possible.

Dream of the Dancing Lamas

Another vivid and powerful dream carried a significant message for me. The dream took place in the open court outside Rumtek Monastery in Sikkim. Sikkim is a small country full of beautiful landscapes, located between India, Bhutan and Tibet. After H.H. the 16th Karmapa fled Tibet, Rumtek monastery in Sikkim became his main seat outside of Tibet. The monastery is located on a mountain, and is surrounded by the natural beauty of mountains, rivers, and wildflowers. In the dream nine lamas were dancing a sacred lama dance in a space cleared especially for them, while a crowd of thousands looked on in great happiness.

I was number nine of this lama group, with no one behind me. We were arranged from largest to smallest, with the largest being the most powerful and beautiful of the lamas. He led the dance, and we followed, our movements all completely synchronized and comfortable.

The largest lama had a very long, white beard that reminded me of Indian Sikhs, and a voice spoke to me, saying it was His Holiness the Karmapa.

When I awoke from the sacred dance of my dream, I realized I had been inside the Mandala of His Holiness the Karmapa, and the dancing lamas were of the Karma Kagyu lineage. I felt a conviction in my heart-mind that once again confirmed I belonged in the Kagyu lineage.

Later, I learned that the 2nd Karmapa, Karma Pakshi, did indeed have a beard such as the one in my dream. Looking back at this dream after I had been empowered and authorized by H.H. the 16th Karmapa shortly before his passing, I realized perhaps part of the dream's significance was that I would be the last lama empowered by H.H. the 16th Karmapa as his representative.

I'm Pointed Towards Rumtek Again

The many experiences and dreams I'd had in retreat contained important messages for me, but when I completed my retreat I still wasn't completely sure what to do. Ven. Beru Khyentse Rinpoche's monastery offered me a position as abbot, but my heart told me to enter another three-year retreat. After all, it had been the best and most wonderful time of my life, and deepening my peace and wisdom even more felt like a valid and skillful thing to do. In the three years of retreat my retreat mates and I had devoted ourselves completely to spiritual development, not creating any negative karma through body, speech or mind. I'd had the auspicious fortune to receive teachings, guidance, and empowerments from Ven. Beru Khyentse Rinpoche and Ven. Kalu Rinpoche. Also, I had been extremely inspired by the great practitioners I had met—many who were devoted to 20-year,

30-year, or even lifetime retreats. These weren't the yogis of some legend, but great beings I had actually studied and practiced with. But since my father had died, I was eager to make the journey to south India to be with my mother and family.

I traveled to South India and arrived at my mother's, and while I was there, we had lunch with my family's long-time lama, the Venerable Bayou Rinpoche, who mentioned casually that H.H. the 16th Karmapa was about to begin a summer retreat at his monastery in Sikkim. Immediately, my mind shot back to the enigmatic invitation I'd received from H.H. the Karmapa seven years earlier. It didn't take me long to sense that there was something auspicious about Rinpoche mentioning the retreat, and that now was the time to complete the puzzle of the invitation and travel to Rumtek.

The community of Tibetan refugees in South India where my parents lived and worked for many years.

The Invisible Man

I was so determined and enlivened by my decision that I didn't even bother applying for a passport so I could legally pass into Sikkim. That would have taken much too long. Instead, I left almost immediately, traveling by bus and train from South India all the way to Sikkim with a single handbag. I wore a Karmapa badge on my shoulder and sat quietly. The problem was that the bus passed through two checkpoints between India and Sikkim. At the first checkpoint, the guard walked up and down the aisle checking passports. I was a little nervous. How would I convince him to let me stay on board without a passport? Yet, miraculously, somehow the guard didn't even see me. He simply walked on by.

At the next checkpoint, the guards started through the bus again. I wondered if I could make myself invisible again. This time a guard did approach me, but I think he must have noticed my Karmapa badge, because he asked me in Nepalese, "Are you from Rumtek?" Now, if I were to answer, he would have immediately heard my strange accent (since I didn't speak Nepalese) and my journey would be in trouble, so I simply nodded my head and showed my teeth with a nice big smile. Satisfied, the guard passed on without asking for my passport. I was on my way to Gangtok, the capital of Sikkim.

A King's Welcome

When I arrived in Gangtok I met up with some relatives of Bayou Rinpoche. They welcomed me warmly when I explained my situation and connection to Rinpoche. My good fortune seemed to be coming in bunches: it just so happened that the very day after I arrived they were headed to H.H. the Karmapa's monastery for his birthday celebration. I would be able to travel with them.

After some travel in the car, we reached the mountain on which Rumtek monastery sits so majestically and began zig-zagging our way up the narrow mountain road. We were taking it nice and slow, when suddenly we heard sirens and commotion behind us. A whole parade of VIPs were right behind us, on their way up to H.H. the Karmapa's birthday celebration. Unfortunately, the road was much too narrow for us to let them pass, so we just continued on, leading the procession.

The scene as we approached the monastery was a marvel. Beginning about a quarter-mile from the front gates, monks lined the road. As soon as our car was in sight, they began to play traditional auspicious welcoming music. We made our way along the rows of monks and through the gates. The car pulled up into the courtyard, stopped, and some monks came and opened my door for me (though they stepped away and moved on to the next car when they saw we weren't VIPs). As I stepped out of the car, I glanced up and saw H.H. the Karmapa and his entire entourage up in the balcony welcoming the arrivals as well. Standing in front of Rumtek in the midst of such auspicious circumstances, with the music and the monks and high-ranking lamas, and His Holiness himself present, was like a powerful ray of sunlight shooting through me. The beauty of this moment is alive in me to this day. Of course they had mistaken us at that point for VIP guests—like high government officials or something—but the welcome nonetheless had an important effect on me. This special coincidence left an impression on my heart-mind and marks an important event on my spiritual journey.

Before I left South India my mother said she had a nephew in Rumtek who might be able to help me once I got there. So as soon as all the guests and VIPs from the parade of cars made it into the monastery, I began to ask for my mother's nephew, the Venerable Thrinley Paljor. Some monks went in and brought out a very round and shiny-headed but handsome lama. He shook my hand,

and said a few things that showed he had already heard a bit about my studies and practice. He was a tutor to a tulku at the monastery—the Venerable Drungrum Gyaltrul Rinpoche. He invited me to his room where we sat to have tea with the tulku and talk. Not far into our conversation we heard the gong ring throughout the monastery—it was time to enter the main shrine for darshan (receiving of blessings) with H.H. the Karmapa on his birthday.

H.H. the Karmapa's Miraculous Memory

I immediately joined the thousands of people who were lined up to approach H.H. the Karmapa's high throne to make an offering and receive a blessing. Just like seven years before, I patiently followed the line as this long string of people made its way past His Holiness. Little by little the line grew shorter and I got closer and closer to His Holiness.

And also like seven years before, something quite unexpected happened as I approached H.H. the Karmapa. I was under his throne, making my offering, and to my astonishment, he bent down from his high seat and spoke to me once again! "Have any trouble on the way up?" H.H. had a serene smile on his face. I smiled and replied, "No sir!"

Once again, I stood for a moment off to the side to watch and see if H.H. was talking to everyone. He wasn't. I confess that for a moment my ego was inflated by this unique treatment. But on a deeper level, in my heart, I felt as though H.H. had been guiding and watching me with his omniscient eye the entire journey.

His Holiness the 16th Karmapa -- Rangjung Rikpe Dorje.

H.H. the Karmapa's Summer Retreat

After the birthday celebration in the main shrine, I was having tea again back in the Venerable Thrinley Paljor's room. Out of the blue, one of H.H. the Karmapa's attendants approached me. "Are you the new lama who has just arrived?" he asked. "His Holiness demands that you enter the Summer Retreat right away."

The retreat had begun three days earlier and it was not customary—in fact it was unheard of—for anyone to be admitted late. Nonetheless, under such a request from His Holiness I couldn't refuse. I told the attendant I was honored and humbly accepted.

Not long after this encounter I heard the gongs and ritual music calling the retreatants back into session. Since I was now a participant, I approached the main shrine room. Just as I was about to enter, the Summer Retreat's head disciplinarian monk appeared from no-where and took me by the hand. He walked me into the shrine, right past all the seats occupied by regular monks, and led me directly to a seat among the high-ranking Rinpoches and Tulkus. Realizing what a rare and pre-cious privilege and honor this was, I could only think to myself, "I don't deserve this."

Orders from His Holiness

A few hours into that first session, H.H. the Karmapa's attendant approached me once again and told me His Holiness wished to see me right away. Of course, I happily followed as he led me to H.H. the Karmapa's private interview room. When I entered, His Holiness was seated. I offered three prostrations and sat on the floor in front of him.

His Holiness began to speak: "I'm glad you came," he said. "I would like you to enter the Summer Retreat. While you are here you will be treated like a Rinpoche, so please take your meals from the Rinpoche's kitchen. Also, I would like you to come see me every day, and I want you to make a connection with the four regents of the Kagyu lineage."

His Holiness went on to tell me about some other very specific things I was to do while I was there. First, I was to give classes to the younger monks at the monastery. Second, His Holiness seemed to know I had studied Sanskrit, because he asked me to give a lecture (on Sanskrit) to the whole monastery at the conclusion of Summer Retreat. It was a tradition for the most learned and accomplished monks and lamas at Summer Retreat to display their wisdom by giving lectures throughout the night.

Of course I was completely humbled and startled by such orders from His Holiness. He seemed to have the idea or knowledge that my being there with him at Summer Retreat was very important. And being there in his presence, I too could sense a special importance in this time. I had complete faith in his wisdom, and obediently accepted his every request.

A Miraculous Translation

I entered Summer Retreat and visited His Holiness every day. Our interviews were full of teaching, smiling and laughing, and meditating. To me, every single meeting with His Holiness was a precious and momentous event in itself. Every word, gesture, glance, and breath of His Holiness was a transmission of blessings from the Karma Kagyu lineage.

There are a few meetings, however, that stand out as quite extraordinary. Once, I was called hastily to His Holiness' chamber. A large group of Westerners was visiting and he had chosen me to be the English translator. I had studied a little bit of English, but by no means was I prepared to translate! But I entered the chamber and took a seat below His Holiness. As the interview began the most miraculous thing happened. Not only could I understand perfectly what the Westerners were saying, but when it came time for me to speak in English the words seemed to flow seamlessly right through me from the Tibetan His Holiness had spoken to the English I was speaking to the Westerners. Somehow the blessings of His Holiness temporarily improved my English. Even today, after years living in the United States, I haven't quite returned to that level of proficiency! His Holiness was very pleased after that interview. In fact, I even remember him patting me on the shoulder and saying to his regular translators, who had been watching the whole time, "Now that's how a translator should be!"

A Great Stand-Up Routine

As the end of Summer Retreat approached the time came for me to give the lecture on Sanskrit His Holiness had requested. To make the occasion of the talk even more auspicious, I was asked to give part of the lecture in Sanskrit. Hearing Sanskrit spoken aloud is uniquely auspicious because it was the language of the Buddha Shakyamuni's original teachings, and is often considered a "language of Gods."

As I began my talk, the monastery was jam-packed with monks and lamas. Outside, the local Buddhist community was gathered to hear the talks from loud-speakers. When my name was called I was very nervous and excited—honored to have such an opportunity in the presence of His Holiness. I approached the front, gave three slow and careful prostrations, and began to speak. I was taking my speech very seriously, annunciating clearly and projecting my voice out over the large space. All was going wonderfully until I began the part in which I was to speak in Sanskrit. The thing is, most people— even the monks and lamas—had never heard Sanskrit spoken aloud before. When I began to speak Sanskrit the whole monastery erupted in laughter. The lamas were cracking up. The visitors outside were in stitches. Even the disciplinarian monks had lost it.

Unfortunately, in my serious frame of mind, I took all this laughter the wrong way. It actually made me a bit angry, and I began to raise my voice even louder. This, of course, only roused my audience more. The roars of laughter continued no matter how loud and clear I made my voice. I looked over at His Eminence Jamgon Kongtrul Rinpoche, who was sitting on the high throne, and even he was laughing, but he was also giving me a thumbs-up sign. Finally, as I neared the end of my speech, I noticed H.H. the Karmapa smiling and looking pleased. Up until that moment I was quite upset and bewildered, but my irritation vanished at seeing His Holiness' reaction to my speech.

The next morning while out circumambulating the holy sites I found I had become a bit of in instant celebrity with the locals, who had been listening to my speech through the loudspeakers. Apparently, they had enjoyed it as much as all the lamas within the monastery. They told me how impressed they were and invited me for food and drinks. Of course by now my frustration had subsided and I was grateful for their appreciation.

New Orders

One day before Summer Retreat concluded His Holiness called me to his chambers. I figured this would be like any other of our daily interviews, but when I entered there were several prestigious lamas and eminences present. I scanned the room and noticed a small, decorated throne had been set up right next to His Holiness. I made my three prostrations and sat in my regular spot on the floor, but suddenly all the lamas present began signaling for me to go sit on the small throne. I felt uneasy about taking such a high seat in the presence of

His Holiness, so instead of sitting on the throne, I scooted a few feet closer to His Holiness, hoping that would appease them. But again they signaled for me to sit on the throne, so I had no choice. When I was settled, His Holiness ordered tea and cookies. He asked me to make a tea offering, and when I was finished he made a gesture to his General Secretary, who began to address me:

"His Holiness would like you to represent him in the West." He went on to explain that this was an extremely important request that I certainly shouldn't refuse.

Of course I was a bit surprised, and I hesitated slightly for a couple of reasons. First, I guess I still had the idea or intention that I should enter a second three-year retreat, and then teach and work for the lineage in India. Second, once before—years earlier while I was studying at Sanskrit University—Jean Claude had invited me to France. When I approached my mother about that invitation, she had disapproved very strongly. This gave me some doubts about how she would take a second request about going West. I didn't want to disrespect the wisdom of His Holiness, or express doubts in the presence of his entourage, but I also needed to clarify my hesitations.

"Your Holiness, you have great wisdom and compassion, and if you can see a benefit to sentient beings from this, I will do as you ask. However, I'm a little worried that my mother will not approve, and that she won't allow me to go."

"I will handle your mother!" His Holiness exclaimed. "I know she will let you go." At this, he ordered several gifts to be prepared and brought for my mother. I knew without a doubt that it was Karmapa's great wisdom, not the gifts, that would convince my mother, and I accepted my new role as a representative for His Holiness and the Kagyu lineage in the West.

At this point, His Holiness turned to the eminences and began to speak to them of my special qualities, and why I would be an excellent help to the lineage by turning the wheel of Dharma in the West. "If he can't do it, no one can!" I could only sit and listen in silence, overcome with gratitude and humility from His Holiness' generous words.

Sure enough, later when I delivered the news and gifts to my mother in South India, she responded with great grace and compassion. "I will let you go if His Holiness sees it is best. Even though it means I will not see you much in this lifetime, I have complete faith in His Holiness."

The Bodhgaya Stupa, where I made pilgrimage after
Summer Retreat with His Holiness.

The Mahaparinirvana of His Holiness the 16th Karmapa

After Summer Retreat I was preparing for my travels West and waiting on the travel documents that would allow me to go. I and another lama friend went on pilgrimage to Bodhgaya, which of course is where the Buddha Shakyamuni achieved enlightenment. At Bodhgaya we circumambulated the Mahabodhi Stupa, paid homage to the bodhi tree where Buddha himself achieved parinirvana (passed completely beyond all suffering), and lit thousands of candles as a light offering. For me, this was a time of reflection and praying for wisdom about my new responsibility and journey into the unknown West. During this time, in the presence and energy of this holy place, I had a vivid dream.

I was standing in front of a beautiful white tent. I approached it and peeked in through the door flap. There sat H.H. the 16th Karmapa meditating alone in deep absorption. I thought to approach His Holiness for a blessing, but then decided to wait until he finished his meditation so as not to disturb him. I turned and immediately saw another white tent, equal to the first. I approached this tent and peeked in, and saw another lama sitting in meditation just like His Holiness. "How strange," I thought, "There are no attendants around or anything." Then I turned from the second tent and saw yet another one, equally white and solitary. When I stuck my head in this one to investigate, there was another lama in meditation. This lama looked familiar, though I couldn't quite place him. At this point a voice in my head explained, "They are in mahaparinirvana."

When I woke, the dream was still very much with me. I considered telling my lama friend about it at breakfast. As we were walking to get breakfast, though, we began to hear rumors that His Holiness had passed away in the United States. Of course the power and conviction of my dream rang through me in complete certainty at this point. To this day, I don't know exactly who the other two lamas were, but I have an idea. About a week after His Holiness passed away a tutor of H.H. the Dalai Lama, who was very close to H.H. the Karmapa, passed away. This may have been the lama I recognized in the third tent. Within a year of His Holiness' passing a high Nyingma lama passed away, and that may have been the lama from the second tent.

Rumtek Monastery in Sikkim, during the cremation ceremony for His Holiness the 16th Karmapa. We observed many miraculous signs.

Witnessing Miraculous Signs

After the vivid dream and news in Bodhgaya I headed back to Rumtek to attend the cremation ceremony of His Holiness.

At the ceremony, thousands of devotees and faithful pilgrims surrounded Rumtek monastery as the smoke from His Holiness' cremation rose gracefully into the blue sky. Thousands of us witnessed miraculous signs, such as spontaneous rainbows and an image of His Holiness' face in the sky. The body of His Holiness left many relics of various colors. One of the most dramatic miracles that day was a rain of delicate flower petals that dissolved at the touch of your hand. These are all signs that manifest for the benefit of sentient beings to indicate that a being has reached perfection on his spiritual path, and it only confirmed what we knew in our hearts from his living presence.

I was filled with sadness that this bodhisattva of unending generosity and compassion was no longer present in the form we knew as the 16th Karmapa. But I was also overcome by great bliss and devotion. My grateful heart rejoiced that His Holiness had blessed me so generously with his wisdom and compassion.

A Ticket to Fly

While in Rumtek I had a short meeting with H.E. Jamgon Kongtrul Rinpoche, Khenpo Karthar Rinpoche, Bardor Tulku Rinpoche, and a sponsor from the West who had volunteered to support a lama. Despite the passing of His Holiness, the rinpoches urged me to carry out his request by agreeing to go to the U.S. and live under the care of this sponsor. "I'll see you in New York," I told them. They were quite pleased I had accepted, and in fact they already had my air ticket and travel documents ready. Shortly after this meeting I flew from Nepal to Delhi, from where I would fly directly to New York.

Dream of Entering Paradise

Shortly before leaving India for the West, I had the following dream about entering a paradise—what in Tibet we call Dewachen Shingkham.

I was in a large group of perhaps a thousand people, and we were visiting an ancient monastery with many statues and temples. I was standing in a long line to enter a temple that housed an enormous statue of the Buddha, when suddenly I noticed there were only a few people ahead of me.

Before me was an ancient, golden Buddha of such enormous size I could not reach the throne where he sat. A monk was handing out incense and bardo lamps, and I knew he was the caretaker and guard for the statue. He gazed at me as I did prostrations, and when I had finished, he came forward to speak to me.

"Do you want to look completely?" he asked. "I can show you." When I replied that yes, I would like to look completely, he pushed a button to open a very small door in the base of the statue. I crawled on hands and knees through the smooth, narrow tunnel.

I suddenly emerged into what I knew must be the other side of the universe. The landscape that met my eyes seemed to glow from within, so radiant were the colors. Flowers the size of umbrellas grew around a crystal-clear lake, and the lotuses that grew from the water were so large a man could walk on them. The sky was turquoise and brilliant with sun, even though a gentle rain fell, and rainbows of many different sizes appeared in all directions. Giant white cranes danced on the shore of the lake.

I was happy to witness this incredible beauty, but knew I must be careful. A voice had told me to beware of the abundant water that collected as dew in the huge flowers. Should the giant leaves shift, torrents of water would wash down on me. Also, the mangoes and bananas were larger than any one person could eat, and I felt a sense of attachment because they looked so delicious.

A voice told me this was Dewachen Shingkham—a glimpse of paradise.

Sherab Ling Monastery, India -- Seat of H.E. Tai Situ Rinpoche

Birthday celebration of H.E. Tai Situ Rinpoche at Sherab Ling Monastery.

Part 6: Into the West

All You Can Eat, All You Can See

The year was 1981, and my first stop in this new world of the West was La Guardia airport in New York City. Some members of New York KTC—a local Kagyu Buddhist group—were at the gate to welcome me. Since they had never seen me before, I remember how they held up a sign with the auspicious Tibetan letter "ah" so that I could find them among the crowd. How astounding that busy airport seemed to me. It buzzed with people and activity as if it were a city in itself.

Outside the airport my amazement only grew. Endless streams of shiny, colorful cars seemed to flow from every direction. In particular, there was an army of bright yellow taxis as busy as a hive of worker bees. There were horns beeping, people shouting, and the roar of planes zooming by right overhead. In the distance the towering skyscrapers of New York greeted me, erect and proud of their kingdom of metal, concrete and noise.

For better or for worse, one of my very first experiences in the United States was a Chinese Dim Sum restaurant, right after leaving the airport. I must have looked quite hungry when I stepped off the plane because that is the first place my hosts took me. The waiters brought cart after cart of all foods imaginable. What really got me, though, was that there were thousands of people in that single restaurant. The noise was incredible. What a fascinating feast! A Dim Sum restaurant has an interesting system: At the end of the meal they come by and count the number of plates you have stacked at your table, and that is what you pay for.

I participate in the Consecration Ceremony of Karma Triyana Dharmachakra, NY.

Breaking Ground at KTD

From the airport we went straight to Karma Triyana Dharmachakra (KTD), the main Karma Kagyu Buddhist center in the U.S. that H.H. the Karmapa's followers had already established near Woodstock, New York.

I arrived at an auspicious moment. H.E. Gyaltsab Rinpoche and other lamas were about to break ground to begin construction on a brand new monastery that would become the official seat for His Holiness in North America. I was pleased and happy to take part in the ceremony. (Today, of course, the monastery at KTD is a thriving center of Dharma activity.)

After the ceremony I spent a few pleasant days at the KTD center. I interacted with the local Tibetan community, met with other lamas and relaxed. It was pleasing to find friendly and even familiar faces shortly after arriving in a new country. Coming to the West was not so bad after all, I thought to myself. I was wrong in thinking it would be so difficult. I was actually quite comfortable.

My days of comfort and familiarity were short-lived, however. Some representatives of KTD suddenly explained that I was to continue on to California immediately, where my sponsor was waiting. This was a surprise. I honestly hadn't realized up until then that KTD would not be my permanent home in the West.

Speechless

Not having a translator and having no experience with American customs or culture made this time period challenging in many ways. When I was asked to give a blessing or perform a ritual, I had no way to ask even simple practical questions, such as "Should I eat before I go?" or "Will you give me a ride home?" Since I wanted to show respect to my new hosts, I hesitated in asking too many questions out of fear of seeming impolite.

But aside from these simple practical challenges, I was struggling to see how I was "teaching" Buddhism to my Western students. For my first three or four years in California, I would simply recite a text in Tibetan by myself, recite some mantra with the students, meditate for awhile, and then smile and say goodbye. With no English and no translator, what else could I do? Sometimes it felt as though my personal motto was, "Eat salad, laugh and smile!"

Back to School

The time came for me to make a very important decision. The way I saw it, I could either study English and become self-reliant, or I could abandon the whole project and return to India and enter another retreat. In my heart, I felt the great faith His Holiness had in me. It was a difficult inner struggle, but in the end it was my faith in Karmapa's wisdom that I rested in. I decided to stay and find a solution to the struggles I faced in my new home. At about this same time, some of the Western students I had made a connection with were encouraging me to study English, which made the decision a little bit easier. In particular, one very generous student named Claire Burnham offered to pay for my classes.

So, with Claire's help, I enrolled in English as a Second Language classes at a local community college in Santa Cruz. At first I think the hardest part was figuring out how the public bus system worked, but eventually I overcame all these logistical problems and my study increased and increased. Eventually I began taking classes at other colleges as well, in Long Beach and San Diego. I enjoyed interacting with my classmates, although there was some cultural discomfort at first. In the beginning I went to class in my full lama robes, and I believe this caused some difficulties with some of my Western classmates. In time, though, I think they saw I was an open, positive person, and they began to enjoy my company as well. "Why are you so happy every day?" they would ask me.

I continued to study several years with Claire's generous financial support, and I eventually graduated from the ESL program and began taking regular courses in English and Comparative Religion. Finally, I reached the point where I could speak with my students in English. As this connection with students grew, I became more confident and skilled in teaching in English, and a larger group of faithful students began to develop around me.

After four years of studying English and adapting to my new country, I must have begun to earn a little attention and respect, because I began to receive invitations from centers and organizations all over the US to come and give talks and teachings.

Signs of Progress

There were a few good signs that I had begun to overcome the language and cultural barriers that had barricaded me and that I was finally connecting with my new brothers and sisters in the West. For one, the professor of my Comparative Religion class learned I was a Buddhist lama, and asked me to contribute my wisdom to the class by teaching and lecturing certain lessons. Shortly after I was also invited as a guest lecturer at UC Santa Cruz in what became an annual opportunity to contribute to Dharma in the Western academic world.

I felt both great exhilaration and humility as my role as a spokesperson for the wisdom of Tibetan Buddhism continued to grow. I became an annual guest speaker at Chogyam Rinpoche's Vajradhatu Retreat in San Francisco, as well as a speaker at New York KTD's Buddhism and Psychotherapy dialogue. I was also deeply honored to participate in H.E. Jamgon Kongtrul's Buddhist/Christian dialogues at Naropa University in Colorado.

In fact, one of my most memorable experiences in the West was a very precious period of time I was able to spend with H.E. Jamgon Kongtrul. I had been asked to coordinate his schedule of teachings, talks, and empowerments during one of his visits to California. Tens of thousands of people would attend and I was honored to hold such a responsibility. During this time H.E. very generously gave me lots of his personal time and attention, and for the first time in many years I felt as though I could share with someone who could understand my unique experience and struggle in bringing Dharma to the West.

He listened with attention and respect when I shared with him many of my dreams and visions for spreading Dharma and benefiting beings. For example, I told him how I felt that advanced university students should complete three more years of study beyond the Archarya degree. I shared with him my dream of opening nursing homes in which the elderly could complete their lives in a healthy and positive environment, with the support of lamas and teachers from their lineage. H.E. liked this idea very much and agreed that it would be a skillful project to realize. Finally, I also encouraged H.E. to continue the interfaith dialogues between Buddhism and other traditions, and this he did until his untimely passing.

Though I know that H.E. Jamgon Kongtrul is a highly realized being beyond birth and death, I was very attached to his last human incarnation, and his passing affected me deeply. Though I know the impression and merit of his many activities continue to benefit beings, I feel in my heart we would all be much better off if he were still here with us. He was deeply loved by all practitioners who ever made a connection with him. His presence and warmth were very magnetic, and perhaps this is part of my own attachment to him. But also, His Eminence understood better than anyone the significance of my connection with His Holiness the Karmapa. He had been present at the summer retreat I spent at Rumtek and

I remember seeing him often. He was even present at the moment His Holiness empowered and authorized me to represent him. His Eminence remembered these things when we were reunited in the West and this helped deepen our relationship.

Because of this strong connection I had developed with His Eminence, I couldn't wait to meet his reincarnation, who was recognized by H.H. the 17th Karmapa himself. I eventually did meet him at Pullahari Monastery in Nepal. He was young, bright, and magnetic, and I had no second thoughts about who he was.

It was flattering that these opportunities continued to increase, but I always prayed with sincerity and devotion that all this activity would genuinely serve H.H. the Karmapa and the Kagyu lineage by spreading the true Dharma that alleviates the suffering of all beings.

With Shambhala Kasung and H.E. Jamgon Kongtrul Rinpoche, practicing archery.

With His Eminence Jamgon Kongtrul in California. (Image at bottom inserted for reference.)

With H.E. Jamgon Kongtrul Rinpoche -- (1984, Marpa House, Boulder, Colorado).

The reincarnation of H.E. Jamgon Kongtrul Rinpoche.

I made strong connections with a Sufi Organization in California. (Image at bottom inserted for reference.)

H.H. the 16th Karmapa with Joe Miller.

Me with the leaders of the Sufi Organization, Joe and Gwen Miller. Joe impressed me with his deep and direct spiritual understanding.

An Encounter with the Sufis

I even had the fortunate opportunity to connect with a Sufi organization in California. I developed a strong relationship with the leaders of this Sufi group, Joe and Gwen Miller. No Westerner had ever impressed me quite like Joe for his depth of direct spiritual understanding. He and I shared many insights and wisdoms from our unique traditions. We advised and counseled each other as trusting friends. I remember he once told me, "You have what sentient beings need. Just offer it to them and you have nothing else to worry about." In the beginning I understood these words only intellectually, but as the years have passed I have come to feel them more deeply, and am grateful for Joe's wisdom. I'll never forget Joe's favorite song of realization:

> "Imagine not,
>
> Think not,
>
> Analyze not,
>
> Meditate not,
>
> Reflect not,
>
> Stay in the natural state,
>
> To be in the essence of mind itself."

I attended many of their annual retreats and enjoyed participating in their spiritual journey. Before Joe passed away he asked me to keep an eye on his followers, and to this day I visit them once a year. I do believe that I have fulfilled my commitment to Joe by overseeing his followers, especially in terms of their spiritual development.

A Lama Drowns in the Sea

On these visits to other centers I built strong connections with new students, and felt like I was finally getting comfortable with Western culture. This allowed me to loosen up a bit, and begin having a little fun. Once, while visiting a center in San Diego, I was with a very close friend named William Bradshaw at a busy beach. We walked up and down the beach, enjoying the perfect temperature and refreshing waves. At one point, I waded out into the water and pretended to be floating face down. I knew this would get my friend's attention because he was already worried that I couldn't swim, and he felt responsible for me. I was right. My friend went into a panic, dove into the sea, and pulled me out of the water to shore. When he had me laid out on the beach as if he was about to do CPR or something, I opened my eyes and asked, "What are you doing?" His face turned the color of a lama's robes, but once he had worked through his anger we both had a great laugh.

These kinds of relationships with new Western students were important, because they helped me gain a deeper understanding of the needs of people in the West. By generating compassion and applying whatever wisdom I had gained in my years of study and practice, I was able to bring the healing and liberating effects of my Tibetan tradition to the people of the West.

My Dharma students in California.

Wedding picture of myself, Tashi Chotso, and my long-time friend William Bradshaw.

Finding the Perfect Companion

In 1996 I met a bright, kind, and beautiful Tibetan woman named Tashi Chotso. We immediately liked each other very much; not only that—somehow we both knew we were meant to be together. In the beginning we were both a bit skeptical about making the commitment of marriage—especially Tashi Chotso. In fact, it took several years, but our similar spiritual outlook and devotion persisted and gave us much in common, and is probably what brought us together so auspiciously.

Aside from this spontaneous connection, there were many aspects of her life story that reminded me of my mother's life story, and this is another factor that probably brought us together.

With the help of my long-time friend William Brad-shaw, Tashi Chotso and I were married in a small town in Nevada (in the Southwestern U.S.). The actual ceremony took place at about 10:00 a.m., and was over within 10 or 15 minutes. It was a far cry from the elaborate ceremony we would have had in a traditional Tibetan wedding! In fact, we didn't even consult the astrological calendar in choosing a date, which is common in Tibetan marriages. However, our simple, humble wedding was the most skillful way for us to marry—thousands of miles from our families—and it was all we needed to confirm our vows and commitment.

I still believe that the ideal situation for a Buddhist practitioner is to live as an ordained monk or nun in accordance with the Vinaya Sutra. However, the modern world often makes this difficult and in the end your practice is about applying the most skillful means you can to your circumstances. So in the case of a practitioner living outside the vows of ordainment, I believe making the commitment to marriage is better than making no commitment at all.

The birth of our daughter Tashi Dolkar brought us many experiences of worldly happiness that I never would have imagined. Suddenly, I understood very directly what it takes to bring up a healthy family, including all the demands and challenges put on householders, particularly in a western, industrialized culture such as the U.S.

This insight is extremely valuable to me. In my role as a spiritual teacher I am surrounded by families and lay persons—these are the beings I am trying to help! Without having this experience myself, I never would have understood so deeply their situations and struggles.

Our beloved daughter Tashi Dolkar, at eight-years old.

Myself, Lama Karma, Tashi Chotso, and Tashi Dolkar.

My students Beth Keenan (far right), Bruce Roe (middle) and Michael Carr (far left) stand in front of the Potala Palace in Lhasa, official seat of His Holiness the Dalai Lama.

Part 7: Back to Tibet

Nearly 40 years after I fled my homeland, China began to ease restrictions and their policies regarding Tibetans. Plus, I now held a U.S. passport, which gave me a little more freedom in traveling. All these things came together and in the early 1990s I made the first of several trips back to Tibet.

Praying at the Potala

I took a small group from the U.S. on a pilgrimage to Lhasa, and my first memory of this journey is how small and disappointing the airport was. I think it consisted of a couple of buildings. I remember how hard it was to find a bathroom, not to mention a good cup of coffee. I wasn't expecting another La Guardia or anything, but I guess I had hoped for more from the most important city in Tibet. Perhaps I had been spoiled more than I realized by the U.S., where everything is big and accessible!

On the road from the airport to Lhasa itself, my disappointment soon faded. I began to notice the sheer beauty and clarity of the landscape. The vividness and the tranquility of these surroundings struck me. Some say the altitude has something to do with this. Indeed, Lhasa sits somewhere between 12,000 and 14,000 feet above sea level. I began to slowly inhale and exhale, resting in the good energy of this place, this sacred environment that I had once been a part of.

When we arrived at Lhasa, the disappointment I'd had at the airport returned. The city was quite small, with few accommodations for visitors. To top it off, we were minded by Chinese government officials everywhere we went. Later, I learned that everything we did was monitored.

Fortunately, the striking beauty of the Potala Palace made up for all this and more. It is much more vivid than you can imagine from just looking at pictures or movies. There in its presence, I realized how special and sacred a moment that was. I was in the capital of Tibet, at the seat of H.H. the Dalai Lama. I let my heart open, hoping the blessings of this holy place would penetrate me deeply.

Although we were being led and minded by a tour guide, we circumambulated the palace, and stopped and did prostrations at different shrine rooms. I was overjoyed at seeing so many holy objects and statues. I didn't think there existed such a collection of ancient statues and relics anywhere on earth. I knew then that the Potala was very alive as a source of power and Dharma energy. But, I also felt sadness at how few practicing monks there were. Instead of a vibrant community of practitioners, these shrines were surrounded by military guards. A sense of loss for the Tibetan people, and the world, filled my gut.

At one point we stumbled across some Tibetan laborers repairing a leaky roof. It was quite clear from their appearance and clothing that they were not very well nourished or taken care of. They told us they worked eight hours a day fixing roofs around the palace. Despite their grim appearance, their good cheer and radiant optimism overwhelmed us. They were so happy when we approached that they began dancing as they worked. Then they invited us to dance and work alongside them—so another highlight of our visit to the Potala Palace was that we got to help patch a roof and do a little dancing.

We visited the famed Jokhang where there was a spectacular statue of Chenrezik, the Buddha of Compassion. It is said that in the presence of that Jokhang statue all wishes are granted.

As we continued to make our way around the palace we found ourselves at H.H. the Dalai Lama's Summer Palace, Norbu Lingka. As you enter, the lush beauty of the interior seems to melt away all outside problems and concerns. Beautiful wall paintings depicted important moments in the Dalai Lama lineage, including one indicating that H.H. the Karmapa was the refuge lama for one of the Dalai Lamas. This simple sight brought me great happiness. I was filled with joy to see that despite the differences and conflicts between the four schools, they are still able to find a natural harmony and compromise. After all, Lord Buddha is the supreme leader of all lineages.

I receive a blessing from Orgyen Trinle Dorje, His Holiness the 17th Karmapa.

Meeting His Holiness the 17th Karmapa

Shortly after the 17th Karmapa, Orgyen Trinle Dorje, had been identified, I was able to visit Tsurphu, the main seat and monastery of the Karmapa lineage. I was very fortunate to have darshan with His Holiness and receive his blessing in this holy place. In the presence of H.H. the 17th Karmapa, I felt immediately that he was the reincarnation of the 16th Karmapa. He welcomed me just as his predecessor would have, and his features and mannerisms reminded me of the 16th Karmapa. He gave us blessings and transmissions and, though he was a young child, displayed great confidence and wisdom. Whatever doubts many of my students held about the authenticity of the 17th Karmapa melted away in the presence of the young Orgyen Trinle Dorje.

At Tsurphu Monastery, 1993

Group visit with H.H. the 17th Gyalwa Karmapa in India.

Yogis Above Tsurphu

In the mountain above Tsurphu there are many caves, blessed by great practitioners for many centuries. We began circumambulating this mountain and soon came across a holy footprint of Drukpa Kunley embedded in the rock between two crystal-clear streams. This seemed like a great blessing and sign, so at about this point we began to climb up the mountain. At one point we came to a small, difficult opening where it is said that those with good karma can pass and those without enough good karma cannot. Most of us didn't even try, because we knew we had a long way to go!

But as we continued on we found the holy cave of the 3rd Karmapa's mother. This Karmapa once touched his finger to the wall of this cave and created a spontaneous stream of water to benefit future retreatants. There was no one in this cave, but farther on the cave of Karma Pakshi (the 2nd Karmapa) was full of retreatants. We decided not to go in and disturb them, but I did notice that right outside the mouth of the cave there was an extremely steep drop-off. You have to be very mindful when you step out of that cave.

When we arrived back at the 3rd Karmapa's cave on our way down the mountain I told my students to continue on down and head back to Lhasa. I would spend the night in the cave, in mountain retreat, and catch up with them the next day. One student, an American named William Smith, asked permission to stay right outside the cave, so I let him stay, but everyone else headed down.

The view of the surrounding snow mountains was breathtaking. For a long time I sat watching the path of sky birds through the setting sun, and listening to the sometimes delicate, sometimes powerful music of the wind whisking through the mountains. As the sun continued to set and evening came the temperature dropped quite a bit, and I had to invite my student friend in—I didn't want to find him frozen stiff in the morning! We sat chanting and practicing in the clear, intense energy of the cave when suddenly I heard someone speaking to me from the mouth of the cave. At first I was startled: "Who could possibly be speaking to us?" I thought. As I looked more closely I saw a monk. "How did you know we were here?" Frankly, we were shocked at this unexpected blessing. We had no idea that anyone would be living there, so high and isolated above Tsurphu.

"We know you are here and you don't have any food." He replied. Then he offered us some delicious hot soup. "Where do you live?" I asked him. He told me he lived in a nearby cave. When we finished our meal the generous monk headed back out into the cold night.

We spent the night in the sacred energy of the cave and had good dreams. In the morning the monk reappeared with some tea and tsampa. Of course we were again full of gratitude. After breakfast we thanked him and were preparing to leave when all of a sudden several other retreatants approached us. Among them was a very old nun, aided by two younger nuns. As they approached, they looked at me and requested Dharma teachings.

"I don't know any Dharma."

"We know you are the lama." Said the older nun.

"Why don't you go down to the monastery and receive teachings from the high lamas and realized beings there?"

"I'm too old. And besides, we want a teaching from you." I saw there would be no getting out of this one. They handed me a large Dharma text and asked me to begin teaching from it. By this point there were at least 20 retreatants crowded around the mouth of the cave, so even if I had wanted to make a run for it, I would have never made it!

I opened the text and began teaching and providing explanation. The retreatants present seemed to benefit, and by the end they were offering me prostrations and gifts of money.

"Please, I have rich students in America, I don't need your money." I didn't want to take what little these retreatants had to survive, but they insisted on it. It was for their own accumulation of merit, they said.

It turned out that in total there were around 40 retreatants in the caves of that mountain. They survived by begging from the occasional nomads who passed through. They used their food frugally and practiced until it ran out and they were forced to go out and beg for more. This sheer and unwavering dedication to practice inspired me. I thought about the West, where we're surrounded by luxury, wealth, and bounty, and yet it seems a struggle just to make it to the practice cushion. These devoted yogis took nothing for granted. They seemed to survive on their love of Dharma alone.

I was overjoyed at the homecoming I received from my many relatives in Kham.

Ani Normug's family.

With my traveling companions and the Venerable Yonten Gyamtso Rinpoche at Dzato.

My nephew Thuba's family.

A Homecoming in Kham

I traveled with a small group of Western students to the area near my birthplace in Kham. I felt great joy, reuniting with old relatives, and meeting new ones. I could never have imagined the massive homecoming I received.

One very special reunion was with my uncle Özer Chapdak, my father's brother. He had stayed behind when my family fled Tibet, and when I saw him for the first time after being separated for 40 years, I thought for a moment I was looking at my father. Their resemblance was striking. He was overjoyed to see me, and full of stories. He told me frankly about the things he had done to survive the Cultural Revolution of the Chinese. In the aftermath of the Chinese invasion, he had done some things that harmed the rich, and benefited the poor and weak. He wasn't proud of many of his actions, but he wasn't ashamed either. "I understand the Buddha's teachings about good and bad karma," he said, "and I think my actions are about even. In human history we have always made mistakes, and this is what I am."

I was speechless after he opened his heart to me with these confessions, admiring his honesty and bravery at confronting his past. As we continued to talk, I learned many things I had never known about my father.

I had another sweet reconnection with my aunt, Ani Normug. She lived with my parents as part of our family when I was a young boy in Tibet. On the night of our escape, she was devastated to be separated from us. Yet, she had managed to create a good life for herself in Tibet, marrying a Tibetan doctor and raising a happy, healthy family. The most bittersweet part of meeting Ani Normug again was hearing her talk about my mother's struggles, raising her children and tending to all the animals while my father was away on business. My mother had told me some of these stories, but there were many powerful details she had left out, and it touched my heart to hear what my mother had endured for her family. As for me, Ani Normug remembered very clearly how clever and naughty I was as a little boy!

My nephew Tsawo Khamsum and his wife Samten Choekyi.

Another fascinating reunion was with my nephew Tsawo Khamsum. He had grown very successful in family, business, politics, and life in general. He is a generous, charismatic man respected by all.

While in Tibet I heard a story that explains, at least in part, one reason why he gets so much respect. Once when Khamsum was a young man a cougar was spotted near his family's camp. Because these predators can be dangerous to the yak and sheep that are the nomad's livelihood, Khamsum and some friends hiked up into the mountains armed with guns and knives in order to track the cougar down. Eventually they came across not just one cougar, but the whole family, including the mother, father, and cub. The men began to chase the cougars and the animals immediately split up and forced the men to split up and separate as well. It turned out Khamsum was running after the adult male cougar when he suddenly realized that his hands were empty—somehow he had ended up without a weapon! At that moment he felt relief that it was the cougar that was running from him, and not the other way around. However, the creature had hidden in the bushes and was sitting ready to ambush Khamsum. It leaped from the bushes and pounced on him, knocking them both to the ground. Khamsum struggled with his bare hands to keep the cougar from slashing or biting him, but he soon realized that this was a case where he would have to kill or be killed. With one hand he managed to grab a giant rock and, through sheer power and bravery, while holding the cougar off with the other hand, bashed it over the head several times with the rock. He had knocked the life from the cougar. Khamsum was a bit beat up and frazzled but still in one piece.

He decided to carry the cougar back with him, so he lifted it onto his back and began the long walk home. The cougar was so large that half its body dragged along the ground behind Khamsum. He arrived back at camp with the beast, much to the shock and amazement of everyone. I was told that after that episode no one really wanted to mess with Khamsum! That is a striking story of my brave nephew that I'll always remember.

Though seeing family brought me great happiness, other aspects of these journeys to Tibet brought sadness to my heart. In many ways the Tibet I saw now did not reconcile with the sweet memories of my childhood. The Chinese invasion, along with the natural advance of time and a changing world, had transformed both the landscape and the life of the Tibetan people. Seeing all the monasteries that had been destroyed was heartbreaking. Even more tragic to me, though, was the way of life that had been lost. The Tibetan life I remembered was always centered around one's spiritual journey and permeated by Buddha-dharma. This focus and foundation seemed in danger now.

Khamsum and his family.

With the Venerable Salje Rinpoche (seated), Tashi Sokpo (to my right) and others at Khamsum's home.

A painting depicting the stupa we built near my birthplace.
It sits in front of Riwa Barmi Gon monastery. May it benefit beings!

In front of the stupa I commissioned
at Riwa Barmi Gon monastery

Tsawo Tsultrim – in charge of building the stupa in Kham.

New Seeds of Dharma

Reflecting on the condition of the Tibetan people and their rapidly changing way of life, a new aspiration began to grow in me: to replant the authentic Dharma that was fading from my homeland, and create something that would nurture the spiritual life of all Tibetans and bring benefit to beings everywhere. I didn't know yet how this aspiration might manifest.

Then, while in a retreat, I began to have vivid dreams of stupas. I took these dreams as a sign that perhaps I should build one. When I mentioned the idea to some students they were very enthusiastic. Since the stupa idea matched my aspiration to benefit my homeland, I decided to build one in Tibet.

It is very difficult to build a stupa from halfway around the world. It took a lot of bodhicitta practice and immeasurable patience and planning to put the project together. Yet the correct causes and conditions came together. There were some financial supporters in the U.S., and some extremely generous anonymous donations from a friend of mine and a student in Taiwan. This was matched by the extreme diligence and devotion of the local Tibetan community, and through all these efforts, the Dharmakaya Stupa manifested in Kham, at the monastery of my childhood haircutting ceremony. It was also the exact site where a large stupa had stood before being destroyed during the Cultural Revolution.

The stupa we built was consecrated by four distinguished lamas from four different monasteries. Now, it serves as a source of Dharmic energy and blessings, where the locals can circumambulate, prostrate and meditate. Through these activities they can gain merit, wisdom and compassion for all sentient beings, and progress on their spiritual path. That was my goal in building the stupa, and, through the blessings of the three jewels, it was accomplished.

My deep-felt prayer is that the stupa serves as a source of light and hope, peace and renewal, for all sentient beings. Through the merit of this project may the seeds of compassion and wisdom nourish a new generation of Tibetans, and continue to heal the wounds of my battered homeland, and those of the world.

A short break on the long road to Mount Kailash.

The glorious Mount Kailash, also known as Kang Rinpoche.
You can see it on the horizon days before you actually arrive.

Pilgrimage to Mount Kailash

I had another aspiration to fulfill in Tibet—to complete the pilgrimage to Kang Rinpoche, otherwise known as Mount Kailash. In the spiritual geography of Buddhism, Mount Kailash is the sacred and secret center of a great mandala, and the source of many blessings for the pilgrims who circumambulate it. It is a place where negative actions are purified, where pilgrims let go of lost loved ones and, through devotion and prayer, have their wishes fulfilled.

You can see Mount Kailash on a clear day from hundreds of miles away—days before you actually arrive there. It is a beautiful, precious mountain whose impact on me is really beyond words. I began to feel as though it were the center and source of the earth itself. When we arrived in our small group I began to enjoy being in the presence of the sacred energy of the mountain. Part of this was watching and enjoying the elements: the harsh, biting winds making music as they moved across the mountain; the clear, surging waters of streams whose rumbling sounds like the chanting of a hundred lamas.

As Buddhists, we circumambulated the mountain clockwise, but the Bon practitioners went around counterclockwise. The Buddhist and Bon pilgrims seemed about equal in number when I was there. With fortune, and the help of sherpas, horses, the ever-dependable yaks, everyone in our group completed the 32-mile circuit around the mountain, completely by foot, confronting vicious winds, sucking the thin air of 18,000 feet above sea-level, and skimming the edges of bottomless crevasses.

The eight- or nine-day journey between Mount Kailash and Lhasa was also a special part of this trip. I enjoyed traveling with our small group. We kept a close eye on each other to make sure everyone was doing okay. Something as simple as sharing some medicine or a cough drop, became part of our practice of patience through hardship. I am sure we received benefit and fruition well beyond measure from our pilgrimage

I commissioned this stupa in Southern India.

Karma and Wangdu were in charge of building the stupa in Southern India.

Karma Triyana Dharmachakra, NY – Seat of H.H. the Gylawa Karmapa in North America.

Visiting with Lama Gangga and Khenpo Karthar Rinpoche

Part 8:
The Jolly Lama Looks Forward

Today I am the resident lama for Karma Thegsum Choling Dallas, otherwise known as KTC Dallas. KTC Dallas is a Tibetan Buddhist meditation center belonging to the Kagyu lineage, and is operated as a branch center of His Holiness the Karmapa's KTD monastery in New York.

In my role here I work to meet the spiritual, psychological, and physical needs of my students. New science and research is showing how these three aspects of our being are completely interconnected, so by helping any one of them, you are affecting them all. I try to approach students with an open mind and light heart, and I have especially found that humor is effective in lightening people's suffering. As I've told students before: "I may not be the Dalai Lama, but I'm the jolly lama!" Laughter and humor help connect us to one another and build trust. This is important if we are ever going to make it through this!

The Dallas KTC provides weekly meditations and teachings that are completely open to the public, to beings of any status, race, background, or religion. Our goal is simple: to relieve suffering and increase true happiness for beings by sharing the wisdom and techniques of the Kagyu Buddhist lineage.

We also try to reach out more widely to the community, first by being good citizens and neighbors. We also participate in interfaith dialogues and celebrations and dedicate the merits of our practice to all living beings.

It has also been important to me to establish a couple of very serious, intensive regular practices at KTC Dallas.

Four times a year we hold the intense purification practice of the thousand-armed Chenrezik, known as Nyungne. We hold a special triple Nyung-ne every year during the auspicious Saka Dawa—the period surrounding the Buddha's birth and enlightenment. It is said that merit accumulated during this period is multiplied exponentially.

Dallas, Texas – USA

Another important regular practice is our annual bluebonnet retreat, named such because it takes place at a secluded camp near Dallas which every year fills with spontaneously blooming bluebonnets. Over the years this week of serious teachings, study, and practice has come to be known as "Bluebunny," for reasons which no one quite understands completely (I've been told it might have something to do with my pronunciation of "Bluebonnet"!).

With students at the 2005 "Bluebonnet Retreat."
Over the years, this week-long retreat has come to be know as "Bluebunny."

The KTC membership is growing, and the number of people attending teachings and practices is always growing as well. To me, this is a clear sign that our activities here are beneficial to sentient beings. If not, I think we would be slowly disappearing rather than growing.

Undertaking a serious spiritual path or practice, such as the Buddha-dharma, is the best way to benefit not just oneself, but all living beings, which of course are limitless. In the 21st century, science, progress, and technology have given us nearly every luxury and convenience in terms of our material lives. Here in the West at least, what more could we really ask for?

However, despite this material abundance and all the benefits of technology the simple state of contentment still eludes us. We feel unhappy, unsatisfied—as if something very important were still missing. This kind of suffering comes from a lack of understanding of the nature of our mind, which in essence is basic goodness.

Uncovering this basic goodness and freeing it from the clinging of ego, and from the poisons of anger, attachment, and aversion is the path to liberation taught by the Buddha. As we work towards this liberation, however slowly or quickly our karma and circumstances allow us, we must hold in our hearts the wish to free all sentient beings from their suffering as well. In Buddhism this kind of love is known as bodhicitta. When we have our hearts and minds set on this cause, so much bigger than ourselves alone, we can overcome great obstacles. If nothing else, I hope my story has shown this: bodhicitta is the most powerful force on earth, and we each have an unlimited supply, waiting to be released from our hearts and minds.

~ Appendix A ~
~ *Tibetan Words and Phrases* ~

~~ PLACES ~~

Dopo Gonpa (a Kagyu monastery in Nepal) [[rDo-Po-dGon-Pa]]

Dzato (a town in Kham) [[rDZa-sTod]]

Jokhang (a famous temple in Lhasa) [[Jo-KHang]]

Kang Rinpoche (Mount Kailash – a famous mountain in western Tibet) [[Gangs-Rin-Po-CHe]]

Karma Thegsum Choling (a Karma Kagyu meditation center) [[Ka.R/Ma-THeg-gSum-CHos-Gling]]

Kham (the wild region of eastern Tibet) [[KHams]]

Lhasa (the capital city of Tibet) [[lHa-Sa]]

Norbu Lingka (the Dalai Lama's summer palace) [[Nor-Bu-Gling-KHa]]

Pa-ji-ri (a large mountain in Kham) [[P/'a-Ji-Ri]]

Potala (the palace of the Dalai Lama) [[Po-T/'a-La]]

Pullahari (a monastery in Nepal) [[Pu.L/La-Ha-Ri]]

Riwa Barmi Gon (a monastery in Kham) [[Ri-Wa-Bar-Mi-dGon]]

Rumtek (Karmapa's seat in Sikkim - a monastery) [[Rum-bTegs]]

Sherab Ling (a monastery in India) [[SHes-Rab-Gling]]

Tso Pema (a famous lake) [[mTSHo-PaD/Ma]]

Tsuphu (a monastery near Lhasa) [[TSHur-PHu]]

~~ PEOPLE ~~

Ani Normug (my aunt) [[A-Ne-Nor-sMug]]

Ashi Gakyi (my sister) [[A-ZHe-dGa'-sKyid]]

Bar[wai] Dor[je] [Chok]tul[(ku)] Rinpoche (a principal lama at KTD monastery in New York) [['Bar-Ba'i-rDo-rJe-mCHog-sPrul-Rin-Po-CHe]]

Bayou Rinpoche (my family's long-time lama) [[Bag-Yod-Rin-Po-CHe]]

Beru Khyentse Rinpoche (a high lama in the Karma Kagyu lineage) [[Be-Ri-mKHyen-brTSe'i-Rin-Po-CHe]]

Bokar Rinpoche (a high lama in the Karma Kagyu lineage) [['Bo-dKar-Rin-Po-CHe]]

Chenrezik (the bodhisattva of compassion) [[sPyan-Ras-gZigs]]

Cho[kyi] Gyam[tso] Trungpa Rinpoche (a Tibetan master who taught extensively in the US) [[CHos-Kyi-rGya-mTSHo-Drung-Pa-Rin-Po-CHe]]

Chodun Dorjee (my mother) [[CHos-sGron-rDo-rJe]]

Drukpa Kunley (a famous wandering yogi) [['Brug-Pa-Kun-Legs]]

Drungrum Gyaltrul Rinpoche (a tulku at Rumtek) [[Drung-Rum-rGyal-sPrul-Rin-Po-CHe]]

Geshe Yeshe Thubten (a teacher at Sanskrit University) [[dGe-bSHes-Ye-SHes-THub-bsTan]]

Guru Rinpoche (he was an early bringer of Buddhism to Tibet) [[Gu-Ru-Rin-Po-CHe]]

Gyalwa Karmapa (the reincarnating head of the Kagyu lineage) [[rGyal-Ba-Ka.R/Ma-Pa]]

Jamgon Kongtrul Rinpoche (one of the 16th Karmapa's 4 regents) [['Jam-mGon-Kong-sPrul-Rin-Po-CHe]]

Kalu [Kyabje] Rinpoche (a high lama in the Karma Kagyu lineage) [[K/'a-Lu-sKyab-rJe-Rin-Po-CHe]]

Karma Chokyip (one of my brothers) [[Ka.R/Ma-CHos-sKyab]]

Karma Pakshi (the 2nd Karmapa) [[Ka.R/Ma-Pa.K-SHi]]

Karma Tsultrim (my father) [[Ka.R/Ma-TSHul-KHrims]]

Karmapa [Rangjung] Rigpe Dorje (the 16th Karmapa) [[Ka.R/Ma-Pa-Rang-Byung-Rig-Pa'i-rDo-rJe]]

Karmapa Orgyen Trinle Dorje (the 17th Karmapa) [[Ka.R/Ma-Pa-Ao-rGyan-'PHrin-Las-rDo-rJe]]

Karmapa Rangjung Dorje (the 3rd Karmapa) [[Ka.R/Ma-Pa-Rang-Byung-rDo-rJe]]

Khampa Gepo (potential adoptive father in Nepal) [[KHams-Pa-rGas-Po]]

Khamtrul Rinpoche (a well known lama who was at my father's cremation) [[KHams-sPrul-Rin-Po-CHe]]

Khenpo Kar[ma]thar[chin] Rinpoche (the abbot of KTD monastery in New York) [[mKHan-Po-Ka.R/Ma-mTHar-PHyin-Rin-Po-Che]]

Khenpo Yeshe Chodar (the Kagyu abbot of Sanskrit University) [[mKHan-Po-Ye-SHes-CHos-Dar]]

Lama Dodhy Rinpoche (my retreat master) [[Bla-Ma-mDo-sDe-Rin-Po-CHe]]

Lama Dudjom Dorjee (the resident lama at KTC Dallas - me) [[Bla-Ma-bDud-'Joms-rDo-rJe]]

Lama Gangga Rinpoche (the abbot of Dopo Gonpa) [[Bla-Ma-Gang-G\'a-Rin-Po-CHe]]

Sakya (one of the 4 great lineages of Buddhism in Tibet) [[Sa-sKya]]

tar-tok (a thorny fruit) [[Tar-THog]] (?Tibetan spelling may be incorrect?)

tsampa (roasted barley flour) [[TSam-Pa]]

tsang (eagle-like bird) [['TSHang]]

tulku (reincarnation) [[sPrul-sKu]]

tum-mo (inner heat) [[gTum-Mo]]

yak (Tibetan beast of burden) [[gYag]]

zhi-chak (spicy noodles) [[Byis-lCags]]

~ Appendix B ~
~ *Index* ~